A characteristic of Christendom was as professionals who were paid to do ministry and facilitate mission. As Christendom fades, churches are reawakening to the biblical concept of the priesthood of all believers—where ordinary everyday church members have the privilege, honor, and most importantly the call to participate in the ministry and mission of the church. I pray that Derek's book, *Untapped Church*, will be a fresh vision for how non-paid church staff can play vital roles in the ministry and mission of local churches.

Ed Stetzer, Wheaton College

Derek Sanford is on to something big and he tells you about it in his new book, *Untapped Church*. It's a game changer! You understand the importance of raising up volunteer leaders, but Derek will inspire you and show you how to reach the potential of high-capacity volunteer leaders that function as staff members. Through story and practical principles this may be the breakthrough book for you and your church!

Dan Reiland, Executive Pastor, 12Stone Church, Lawrenceville, GA.
Author of *Confident Leader*!

If you are looking for ways to take your volunteers to the next level, you'll definitely want to read *Untapped Church: Discovering the Potential Hidden in Your Congregation*. I hope you'll go on this journey with author Derek Sanford to learn how to unleash the high-capacity potential in your church to serve for greater impact. Untapped Church is what you're looking for in this next ministry season.

Dave Ferguson, Lead Visionary - NewThing
Author - *B.L.E.S.S. 5 Everyday Ways to Love Your Neighbor and Change the World*

You don't have to hang around a group of pastors long before you sense the only thing holding them back is that their particular church is under-resourced. But is it? What if the Apostle Paul's words to the church in Philippi were still true for all church leaders today? What if God has already supplied us with all we need to have an impactful church? With words and authenticity that only come from a seasoned and experienced leader, in *Untapped Church*, Derek Sanford dismantles the myth of the under-resourced church. With practical steps and real-life examples, Derek demonstrates how God truly has supplied each church with all that is necessary to become a healthy and contributing part of the body of Christ. Following Derek's example, may we dare to dream of what might happen if only we would unleash all of the potential that God has already placed within our churches.

David Ashcraft, Senior Pastor, LCBC Church

I'm not sure there's a more important leadership understanding than how to invest in and serve volunteers. Pastors and leaders [who] ignore the most important resource they have will never move the ministry as far as they could. My friend, Derek Sanford, is one of the best equippers of volunteers I've ever seen. So listen up to an amazing leader as he equips YOU with skills to do the same in his new book *Untapped Church*!

Tyler Reagin, Founder and CEO of the Life-Giving Company and Author of the new book *Leading Things You Didn't Start*

UNTAPPED CHURCH

DISCOVERING the POTENTIAL HIDDEN in YOUR CONGREGATION

By

Derek Sanford

Contents

Access Additional Resources

Sermon Manuscripts
Discussion Questions for Each Chapter
Team Exercises
www.dereksanford.com

Introduction

Why Write This Book?

In 2015, I visited Dan Reiland at 12Stone Church in Atlanta, Georgia. Dan served as John Maxwell's right-hand man for two decades. He has authored many great leadership books, including *Amplified Leadership*, and he writes the popular leadership blog called *The Pastor's Coach* at DanReiland.com. Dan serves as the chief of staff at the influential 12Stone Church. The purpose of my visit was to pick Dan's brilliant mind about leadership development strategies for our church and staff. Our time together was incredibly helpful to me and exceeded all my expectations.

But about halfway through our meeting, I began to describe the volunteer leadership culture at my church, Grace Church, just outside of Erie, Pennsylvania. I told him how we have volunteers leading at every level of our organization and that our staff is made up of one-third paid and two-thirds unpaid leaders. When I said that, something strange happened. This leadership guru, one of my ministry mentors from afar, began to ask *me* questions! He was picking *my* brain! In the end, Dan asked if he could do an interview with me for his blog so that other church leaders around the country could benefit from our conversation. Of course, I was willing and honored to oblige. After the blog post was published, I began to get inquiries from pastors around the country about starting a culture of volunteer leadership in their church. Many of them asked me to put our learnings on paper so that others could benefit, and I knew that this book needed to be written.

Audience and Structure

First and foremost, this is a book for pastors. My prayer is that if you are a pastor or church leader, your eyes will be open to the incredible leadership potential that exists in your church. But also, if you are a marketplace leader, I hope that you will be reminded of the power of volunteerism. And finally, if you are a Christian who is attending church but not being used to your full potential in ministry, I hope that you will be inspired by the possibilities of what God might do through you.

This book is structured into two main parts, using Grace Church's story of empowering volunteer leaders throughout. In the first part of the book, I will explore some biblical foundations, philosophical shifts, and real-life stories of leaders who have been tapped for kingdom impact. The second part of the book is much more practical in nature. It has the feel of a how-to manual. Not because these are easy-to-follow steps that will automatically produce the desired result. But I hope to provide replicable principles for other churches and nonprofits who want to develop a volunteer leadership culture. My ultimate prayer is that ministry will be multiplied and Jesus will be lifted up. I hope someone will read these words and take this idea further and make it better than I ever dreamed it could be!

A Snapshot of Grace Church

Let me give you a little introduction to Grace Church (www.whoisgrace.com). We are a multisite church with three locations in the suburbs of Erie, Pennsylvania. We are a very old church, but as we like to say, "We don't act our age!" Grace was founded as an urban house church in 1895 (figure 1) by nineteen Swedish immigrants and has been an active part of the Erie community ever since.

In our pre-COVID multisite reality, Grace McKean was a site of approximately 1,150 people (figure 2). Grace Harborcreek, our second location (launched in 2010), was a site of about 600 people (figure 3). And Grace Girard (launched in 2015) was a site of about 150 people (figure 4).

old church

McKean

Girard

Harborcreek

So overall, Grace was a church of about 1,900 weekend attendees in our physical locations—around 550 of those were members. There were about thirty paid full-time and part-time staff and approximately sixty volunteer staff with over one thousand active volunteers.

As I finish this manuscript, we are still in the throes of COVID-19. Our congregation has moved exclusively online. Like so many other churches and organizations, Grace is continuing to adapt, and things will likely look different by the time this book has been published. However, while details of attendance and operation have fluctuated, the overall volunteer culture remains strong.

Part 1

A Different Kind of Church:

CHAPTER 1

The Great Opportunity

A Compliment . . . I Think

I think something got lost in translation.

Despite the language barrier, on July 6, 2017, I received the greatest pastoral compliment ever given to me. I had been leading at Grace Church for over twenty years, and we were in a season of momentum and expansion. Part of that expansion was adding our third Global Partner—this time Oono Church near Tokyo, Japan, and their incredible leader, Pastor Nobuyuki Nakazawa or as we call him — Pastor Nobu.

Japan represents a huge unreached people group with less than .5 percent of the Japanese population being evangelical Christians. So our churches in Pennsylvania and Sagamihara decided to partner together to share best practices, resourcing, and coaching.

Pastor Nobu had recently sent a representative, Pastor Keisuke Nakazawa (who graciously suggested we call him Pastor K), to visit our church. He had spent a week interviewing, observing, and generally learning about our approach to ministry and our recent growth as a church. Upon Pastor K's return to Japan, Pastor Nobu and I connected for a call. It was 10 p.m. for me and 11 a.m. the next day for him. As I sat at my kitchen table on that warm summer night in my T-shirt doing some last-minute Skype audio and video checks, I was eager to hear about the results of Pastor K's trip to the States. I discovered that he had prepared four hours of lectures to present to his church in Japan about our church in America, and I couldn't wait to hear his first impressions.

I imagined that he was impressed by our beautiful facilities or effective outreach strategies. Certainly, he must have been blown away by my brilliant approach to church leadership and preaching. Oh, you can feel it coming . . .

After our usual greetings— "How is your family? How is the weather? What happened this past Sunday?"—I finally popped the question to Pastor Nobu: "What were Pastor K's impressions of our church?" This question is the equivalent of asking a girl on a first date where you rank on the handsome scale.

His response went something like this: "Here in Japan, when we hear about a megachurch in America, we picture a church where the senior pastor is a famous leader, or a charismatic personality, or a brilliant communicator or author. *But*" —here it comes— "when we visited your church, we found *none* of these things."

Oof! In the moment, I had to stifle my laughter because it was totally innocent but absolutely true—and also, I knew exactly where he was going with this.

He went on to describe the church that I know and love: Grace Church. A church that is known not mainly for the quality of its preaching, or the quality of its worship or excellence in kids' ministry (although our hope is that those things are pretty darned good!), but a church that is recognized by the quality and capacity of its people.

Every church has volunteers, but at Grace we have created a culture where those volunteers can rise to every level of leadership in our organization. For example, we have had a volunteer campus pastor running one of our multisite locations, we have volunteer worship leaders on our stages most weeks, we have had volunteers supervising paid staff, and we have had volunteer leaders on our five-member Strategic Lead Team that drives the entire strategy for our church. In fact, at our full staff meetings, volunteer staff outnumber paid staff two to one.

So to say that Grace Church is not built around my personality, preaching skills, or charisma is a huge understatement. Thank God it's not about me! That's why Pastor Nobu's statement was my biggest compliment. It's one thing to build a big church around a rock-star pastor. But we've built a large, growing, multisite church around the concept that our people are our greatest asset, and they can accomplish more ministry than we ever thought possible.

Early Days

I came to Grace in 1995 as the youth pastor. It was a traditional Baptist church that was growing under the steady leadership of long-term pastor Al Detter. In addition to Pastor Al, the staff consisted of a children's pastor, youth pastor, financial administrator, two secretaries, a worship coordinator, and a cleaning lady.

Al's preaching was solid and biblical and had become a draw within the community. The church was well-organized and structured for ministry to get accomplished. During our weekly staff meetings, we would come together and discuss the ministry that needed to be done that week. What were the scheduling implications? What were the budget implications? How should communication happen? Who is doing what? We covered it all.

Then, each month, various elected committees met to determine how those ministries were to be carried out within the life of the church. The outreach committee covered the details of the women's tea event that would hopefully draw in some new families from the community. The worship committee would work on the roster of musicians for the upcoming month and the setlists for each week of worship. The finance committee would dig into the balance sheets and individual ministry budgets to figure out where cuts could be made so that the monthly budget would come in on track. The missions committee would make sure that our oversees missionaries were properly communicated with and funded. At any given time, there were between six and twelve functioning committees at work. Each staff person had one or more committees that they sat on to make sure all the ministry was well-coordinated with the office. This is how church had operated for many years, and the system worked well.

Pastor Al had done some research and writing on a concept called "mini congregations." Grace was a fairly large church at the time, with between four and five hundred weekend attendees. Mini congregations would provide the infrastructure for discipleship and care, and would also require a new layer of volunteer leadership. These mini congregations would need mini pastors to step up and lead and teach and counsel. Our youth ministry began to adapt a similar model that broke from the mold of committee-based leadership. Instead we employed gift-based leadership. High-capacity leaders were invited to lead, to create, to shepherd.

I remember seeing people come alive as they were invited to participate in ministry at a level they had never experienced before. As a result, they were being used by God in a way that set their hearts on fire. The decision to include them and unleash them were foundational in creating the church that we're experiencing today. Seeds were planted that would begin to grow and blossom decades later.

Untapped

I'm convinced that the greatest untapped resource in today's church is potential high-capacity volunteer leaders who are willing to serve as staff members without pay. Week after week, they sit in the seats of big churches and small churches; urban, suburban, and rural churches; Black churches, white churches, Hispanic churches; and international churches of every stripe. They attend services, they sing, they take notes, they participate in small groups, and may even serve in a ministry. Yet their potential to impact God's kingdom is largely untapped.

Untapped simply means "available but not used."[1] How many people in our churches are available to do great things for God? But they haven't found a ready environment where they could be used. How many ministries are being quenched? How much kingdom impact is being unrealized? How many visions are being suppressed because church leaders haven't created an atmosphere that frees high-capacity leaders to attempt great things for God?

Many church members have very important jobs out in the real world. They spend their days making important decisions, impacting lives, supervising employees, changing the world with their craft. What statement does it send when we recruit them to hand out bulletins, or cue the lighting scenes, or change diapers as their main ministry contribution to the church? Don't get me wrong, as a pastor, I fully understand how critical these seemingly minor roles are. And I also recognize that some of our church members have too much going on in their lives to invest at a leadership level. But I'm afraid that the subtle message that we have sent to our high-capacity leaders when we recruit them to menial church roles is "God's work isn't nearly as important as the secular work that you do in the real world."

Nothing could be further from the truth! The church holds the keys for the restoration of the world. There are far-reaching problems to be solved, life-and-death decisions to be made, and kingdom initiatives to be implemented in every single community around the globe where churches exist. The hope of our planet depends on each local church reaching its highest potential.

Not only are pastors *not* equipped to lead churches by themselves, they are not called by God to do it alone either. God never intended that a select group of professionals called "clergy" should carry the full responsibility of leadership in the church. God's dream was for an army of empowered lay people equipped by paid and unpaid leaders to overwhelm the world with the good news of Jesus' love for humanity (Romans 12:4–8; 1 Corinthians 12:4–7; 1 Peter 4:10).

As one individual pastor, I don't have a broad enough range of expertise to know how to lead well. I don't have the experiences to know what to do about most social justice issues. I don't have the catchy slogans or digital know-how to roll out the next church marketing initiative. I don't have a clue how to counsel someone who is struggling with anxiety. I don't have enough good HR ideas to keep employees satisfied and motivated. I don't have the accounting wherewithal to create and execute a financial plan to keep my church on track. But do you know what I do have? People in my church who are experts at all those things. I believe that many of them are in your church too.

But maybe they're *untapped*: available but not used. What if you tapped into their expertise? Not just as consultants but as partners? In 2011, we at Grace took the next step and started asking high-capacity leaders from our congregation to join our staff without pay. We gave them job descriptions, problems to solve, and people to lead. We gave them responsibility that matched their capacity. And guess what—our church started to take off and take on a whole new identity.

Reversing the Trends

The trends among pastors aren't good. In recent years, we've seen ministry leaders rise and fall at an alarming rate. Pastors are struggling, and many are making career-ending mistakes. Stress levels are through the roof. Anxiety, depression, and anger are epidemic. And for every one pastor's fall from grace that makes it to the news, you can be sure there are dozens of others whose churches were too small to make headlines. But the carnage left behind is no less significant. Being a do-everything pastor is too much pressure for one person. It's too much responsibility—too much spiritual expectation. But what if many pastors are fighting for their lives while a life-giving answer to their problems surrounds them?

There's an old story about a group of Spanish sailors and explorers who were approaching South America after a long and difficult voyage across the Atlantic. Their ships were finally within sight of the coast of modern-day Brazil, but, too weak to paddle and with critical damage to their sails, they found themselves simply floating. They were unable to approach the shoreline. The headwaters of the Amazon River emptied into the ocean up ahead, creating a current that pushed them away from the shoreline and kept them marooned at sea. The current was much too strong to swim, and they had run out of food and water days before. Soon the sailors started dying of thirst. They certainly couldn't drink the saltwater from the ocean, because it would cause dehydration and nausea and would only hasten their deaths.

About this time, another schooner passed by close enough for the Spanish sailors to cry out in distress. They yelled, "Water, water! We need water!" A surprising reply came back from the sailors on the passing schooner. "Cast down your buckets where you are."

You see, there was a critical piece of information that the Spanish sailors didn't know. The Amazon River flows out into the ocean with such a ferocious force, it carries a stream of fresh water up to a hundred miles into the ocean. So let me recast the scene for you, now that we have all the facts: Day after day on the Spanish vessel, men were dying of thirst while they floated on top of the world's largest source of freshwater. Dehydrated while sitting on top of a sea of life-giving water.

This scene is a metaphor for our era—and the state of the modern pastor. I'm convinced that there are pastors all across our country and around the world who are surrounded by freshwater and dying of thirst. Some of you reading this book would count yourself among their number. All you would have to do is cast down your bucket where you are and drink and live and be satisfied. I believe that high-capacity volunteer leaders in our churches are key to help us reverse the trends of pastors burning out and dropping out.

Yet more and more, big churches and small churches view the sole answer to their burnout problem as simply adding more paid staff. In large churches, the trend is moving toward paying more staff. Tony Morgan discovered a rapidly growing staff-to-congregation ratio in his survey[2] of churches. Just fifteen years ago, it used to be that in growing churches, the healthy ratio was 1:100 (one paid staff equivalent for every hundred people in the congregation). In 2017, that ratio was 1:67, and in the first quarter of 2020, it was 1:59. That is a fast and dramatic shift in the number of paid staff in churches. It seems that more and more growing churches are quickly adding paid staff to address their ministry needs. And overstaffed churches are just a few bad decisions or one economic downturn away from a personnel disaster. Talk about stress.

Small churches aren't off the hook. I have spoken with countless small-church pastors who are stuck, discouraged, or otherwise paralyzed because they are convinced the answer to their momentum problem is to hire another staff person. They believe that until they can get the money together to hire that person, they'll just keep doing everything themselves and hope for the best. So those pastors find themselves in every hospital visit, every preservice microphone check, every Sunday school class, every youth overnighter, and every church workday. By committing so much time and energy to such a wide variety of tasks, they aren't spending time on the very things that will help their church go to the next level. Things like leadership development, preparing and preaching great sermons, creating and communicating vision, and planning for the future. Putting their effort into these few things might actually position the church to hire that new staff person, but they will never get there because of the day-to-day chaos.

What if in big churches and small churches alike, the solution is right under your nose? What if, like those Spanish sailors, you are sitting right on top of the life-giving answer? Maybe there are people all around you who are untapped—available but not used. "Cast down your bucket where you are, and you will survive."

Our church decided to start tapping into the untapped greatness that was all around us.

A Face to a Name

I want to introduce you to just a few of our many outstanding high-capacity volunteer leaders who are on our staff. I hope this quick early snapshot will give you an idea of the kinds of roles and time commitments our volunteer leaders are investing. You will find out more about some of these amazing people (and others) throughout this book.

Doris is a retired executive from a large insurance company. She has volunteered ten to fifteen hours per week to oversee our Next Steps ministry. This involves providing direction and oversight to all staff who work on our discipleship ministries.

Sarah is a stay-at-home mom who has provided oversight to our Life Groups ministry and is also on our preaching team. She volunteers ten to fifteen hours per week to oversee all our Life Group leaders and curriculum teams.

Jim is a partner in a local accounting firm and our pastor of staff care. He has also served in providing leadership for all our site pastors. Jim has volunteered fifteen to twenty hours when supervising our pastoral team through regular one-on-one check-ins, strategy meetings, and ultimately annual performance reviews.

Our staff is made up of almost sixty others who are similar to these three. Not everyone works the same number of hours or has the same scope of responsibility, but they have this in common: they are leading other leaders and they are responsible for vital ministries and/or departments in our church.

CHAPTER 2

Are We Allowed
to Do This?

My son Chase had just started to learn to play hockey. He was nine.
We happened to have an NHL player in our small group at the
time. He lived in our area during the off-season but played for the Pitts-
burgh Penguins when the season was in full swing. One year, he secured
some tickets for Chase and me to attend one of the Penguins' home games.
The tickets came with one additional perk. He texted me instructions that
after the game we should make our way down to the locker room to meet
some of the players. This was crazy! I'm not a big hockey guy and Chase
was totally oblivious, but I know a big deal when I see it! We watched a
great game, and in the final minutes, we made our way through the dark
underbelly of Mellon Arena (stadiums change names so often I actually
had to Google that!). We stood at the exit of the locker room—Chase's
eyes were wide and mine were even wider. Players started to emerge, and
we met one star after the other. We even got to see some of the opposing
Philadelphia Flyers. The surprise of the night was meeting Mario Lemieux,
which we found out later was pretty rare.

I'll never forget the rush of anticipation in the moments leading up to
that locker room door swinging open for the first time. But my fondest
memory from that day is Chase looking up at me with his wide blue eyes
and saying, "Dad, are you *sure* we're allowed to do this?"

It's a question that we all ask when we feel like we're in a little over our heads. When you cross the line into the deep end of the pool for the first time. Or when your fifteen-year-old self first sits behind the wheel of a car in an empty parking lot. Are you *sure* I'm allowed to do this? It's a question we asked a lot in the early days of rethinking the paradigm for how the church is "supposed" to work. Putting volunteers into important staff roles always felt a little like breaking some unwritten code. "Will they take it seriously? Can we hold them accountable if they are not earning a paycheck? Will anyone in the congregation really respect them?" These were legitimate questions that we wrestled with, but there were some key factors along the way that kept our team chasing this different way of doing church.

Ownership Fuels Invitation

I got my first glimpse at the power and potential of volunteer leaders early in my ministry experience.

The phrase "going postal" was coined in the mid-'80s and early '90s due to a series of active shooter incidents in which US Postal workers let their work stress bubble over into workplace violence and even murders. It's incredible to think back to that brief time when mailmen were labeled as some of the most violent members of our society. For a while, whenever there was a shooting, especially in the workplace, it was called "going postal."

At that time, I was the youth pastor at Grace. It was my dream job. I was rebuilding a ministry that had been recently rocked by scandal and moral failure. So it was a story of small beginnings, about a dozen faithful junior and senior high school students. I had virtually no ministry experience, but I knew this much: no adult knows how to reach these kids' friends better than they do. We started a biweekly outreach service called INSIGHT that was completely designed, planned, and executed by students. I provided some guidance but gave a lot of creative license to the students themselves, including the writing and directing of our dramatic skits. The aim was to present a timeless biblical truth by acting out a relevant modern scenario.

On one fateful Wednesday night, one of those skits ended with the main character, a mailman, alluding to "going postal" right on the stage of the church. It was culturally relevant, it was edgy, it was satirical, but it was also the last straw for a bunch of families who proceeded to leave the church. To be honest, I don't remember if the biblical punchline of the skit was worth losing people over—maybe not. But I do remember what we gained from that line-in-the-sand moment: We needed to decide whether it was worth it to empower students in major leadership roles or whether we should leave the leading to the grown-ups. We went all-in on student empowerment.

In the heat of the backlash, I doubled down on the idea of volunteer leadership among our students. Yes, we lost some families, but at that point INSIGHT had grown from about 12 attending students to about 250. Why? Because ownership fuels invitation. The more that students owned the ministry, the more likely they were to invite others to be part of it. At the time, some of our more "mature" churchgoers struggled to accept the kinds of students who were walking through our doors. We installed ashtrays on the sidewalks so that kids could extinguish whatever they were smoking before coming into church. All varieties of tattoos and piercings and colored hair were on display every week (hey, it was the '90s), but students were coming to Jesus in droves. And the reason many of them came was that one of their buddies had written the skit, or the girl that sat next to them in chemistry had made a video, or they had to see the competition that the stoner-turned-Jesus-freak came up with for everyone.

Don't get me wrong, we had high expectations from our students in leadership. These high school kids were high-capacity, high-commitment volunteers! Their discipleship expectations were intense; the hours they spent in planning meetings and rehearsals and training was significant. Some students would come straight from school every day and spend hours working in ministry. Our commitment, not just to volunteerism, but to empowering volunteer leaders, threw the doors open to a huge group of kids we wouldn't have reached otherwise. The more ministry the students owned, the more friends they invited to check out Jesus. Our church was reaching unchurched students and their families in droves. It felt like the first time swimming under the rope into the deep end of the pool. It caused me to ask many times, "Are we allowed to do this? Is the church allowed to operate like this? Are pastors allowed to give away huge leadership responsibilities to inexperienced and even unqualified people like high-school students?" I sensed that Jesus' answer was "yes."

Jesus' Example of Empowerment

It seems that Jesus himself sent out his disciples way too soon by our standards. It is likely that many of the disciples were teenagers themselves when they threw down their nets and followed him for the adventure of a lifetime. They would have barely completed the membership class, let alone seminary, by the time Jesus was empowering them with major ministry responsibilities. Remember, these were uneducated, inexperienced young men. They had either dropped out or flunked out of rabbi school, which is why they had pursued careers like fishermen and tax collectors. And these were the very people that Jesus sought out and eventually entrusted with the salvation of planet earth. We can learn from Jesus' empowerment of these twelve greenhorns. Let's observe his four-step approach outlined in Mark 3:14–15:

> And he appointed twelve (whom he also named apostles) so that they might be with him and he might send them out to preach and have authority to cast out demons.

He Selected Them: "He appointed twelve"

Jesus had a selection process. In fact, over in Luke 6:12–13, we get a glimpse at his methodology:

> In these days he went out to the mountain to pray, and all night he continued in prayer to God. And when day came, he called his disciples and chose from them twelve, whom he named apostles.

Did you catch that? *All night* he continued in prayer before choosing his leadership team. Did Jesus really need to pull an all-nighter to get his answer from God? Didn't his divine nature give him an insider's look at the right names? Yes, but Jesus is providing a model for us to follow. He's demonstrating by example that if you try to assign leadership roles without significant prayer, you're making a big mistake. So the critical first step in empowering the right volunteer leaders is to be sure they are hand-picked and vetted in prayer.

He Spent Time with Them: "That they might be 'with him'"

Jesus provided the apostles with the opportunity to acclimate to his ministry. They heard his teachings; they saw his miracles; they participated in private debriefings around evening campfires with their leader. It seems that their time together was reasonably short (maybe only a few months) before they were sent out in ministry. Even so, it is important for our volunteer leaders to spend time with us and become acclimated to our ministry style and goals.

He Released Them in Ministry: "he might send them out to preach"

It is interesting that Jesus involved them in a preaching ministry that was clearly the main goal in *his own* job description. Over in Luke 4, Jesus makes this declaration: "I must *preach* the kingdom of God to the other cities also, for I was sent for *this purpose*" (emphasis added). It was his purpose to preach, yet this was the very task that he delegated to his disciples. If you are a pastor, how long would it take for you to delegate your preaching duties to an untrained, unpaid volunteer leader? Probably more than a few months! Pastors must develop the ability to release our volunteer leaders into ministry sooner than we think.

He Gave Them Authority: "And have authority to cast out demons"

This is key. Jesus gave his disciples not only a task to do but also the authority with which to accomplish it. Luke 9:1 actually says that Jesus gave them both *power* and *authority*. Power is the ability to do a thing. Authority is the right to exercise that power. Obviously, we mere humans don't have the ability to transfer power and authority in exactly the same way that Jesus did. However, if our volunteer leaders are going to be successful in their new roles, there must be a clear transfer of authority from the pastor.

To my lingering question, "are we allowed to do this?" the Bible seems to say yes. In fact, maybe Jesus doesn't just *allow* us to activate a volunteer leadership culture within the church—maybe he *expects* it. It seems like he modeled it himself, and then gave us a ministry pattern to follow as he released his own high-capacity volunteer leaders we call "Apostles." He found a group of unlikely candidates, and then he selected them, spent time with them, released them into ministry, and gave them authority to do what he asked them to do. If this was the example of Jesus, why should we do anything else?

What Is a Volunteer Leadership Culture?

All churches and many organizations and nonprofits have an army of volunteers who do very important work: greeters, ushers, nursery workers, small group leaders, food pantry workers, musicians, peer counselors, and many more. In most cases, these volunteers are led and managed by paid staff. The difference in a volunteer leadership culture is that supervisors at every level are also volunteers. I'm talking about enlisting high-capacity volunteers who are responsible to lead other leaders and volunteers, who will then do the ministry. In fact, if taken to its logical conclusion, in some cases there can even be volunteers supervising paid staff members. Let's use the following as our simple definition:

> Volunteer Leadership Culture: *A culture in which high-capacity volunteers (and not just paid staff) are entrusted with the responsibility of leading leaders.*

As this culture was developing at our church, I remember thinking, "I am giving away important ministries at an alarming rate!" I was entrusting entire programs, entire departments to high-school kids, young adults, and other leaders. As energizing as the whole thing was, we began to notice a strain on the infrastructure that had served us well for many generations. A red-tape-filled decision-making process was hindering our efforts to empower these young leaders. Some of you reading this may not even be able to see the possibility of an empowerment culture because your mind immediately goes to the roadblocks in your own organization. We faced this moment too. We needed to address the roadblocks.

Removing Roadblocks: Two Decisions

As the youth ministry was blowing up, providentially our senior leaders started to remove some barriers that were impeding growth in the church as a whole. There were two major decisions that proved to be critical precursors to a thriving volunteer leadership culture.

Getting Rid of COMMITTEES

In the late '90s, like a good Baptist church, we had committees for everything. We had an education committee, worship committee, missions committee, visitation committee, finance committee, and more. Most important was the nominating committee. This committee was charged with recruiting people to serve on the other committees.

Once a person was recruited, their name would go before the church for election onto the committee, where they would serve for two years. Obviously, this structure wasn't nimble enough to accommodate new and emerging leaders and to quickly onboard them as we grew. So we started to systematically get rid of all those committees, opting instead for a staff-led, team-based church. It wasn't an easy battle, and it came with a lot of power grabs and eventually many disgruntled people leaving the church, but it was absolutely critical in paving the way for us to get the right people in the right ministry roles.

Removing the formal committees and formal processes allowed us to make it easy for people with gifts to use their gifts. They no longer had to wait for the next nominating and election cycle to gain a seat at the table. Along the way, we also realized that the committee system was founded on distrust. It was patterned after a governmental model of checks and balances, instead of biblical principles like trust, shared responsibility, and gifts-based leadership. During a stretch of about five years, we went from eight committees to our current model of one elected team of elders. These leaders still require a congregational vote in order to serve, but they're the only ones. We have found that a staff-led, team-based structure is most effective for growing a church. The committee system was far too restrictive.

In fact, there are some examples in the Bible of decisions being made by committees, and they all turned out bad. "Majority rules" isn't always the best policy. The ten spies won out over Caleb and Joshua in refusing to obey God and occupy the promised land (Numbers 13–14). That didn't turn out well. Joseph's brothers formed an ad-hoc committee and took a vote deciding to throw Joseph into a pit and sell him into slavery (Genesis 37). Things came around for the brothers in the end, but I'm not sure they'd want to repeat the process if given the opportunity. When Moses was gone for too long on the mountain, the Israelites held an "all-church meeting," and the ayes defeated the nays as they decided to worship a golden calf (Exodus 32). The moral of the story: "Church committees are from the devil!" OK . . . I'm kidding (kinda). My point is, we got rid of a bunch of committees, and it was a critical step in allowing our volunteer leadership culture to take root.

Reducing Competing PROGRAMS

We were a typical church in that we had been adding new programs year after year and never had the courage to subtract any. We were whatever is the opposite of "simple church." For a while, we had Sunday night services, Wednesday night family night (with a full meal), women's ministry, men's ministry, midweek kids' ministry, sports ministries, retreats, vacation

Bible school, and on and on. It was a very important day when we began to systematically get rid of all of these competing programs. Not because any of these programs were bad, but because they provided no clear path for people to become more like Jesus. We realized that in order to be more effective as a church, we had to do less. At the same time, the few things we chose to do needed to be done better.

Now, my goal here is not to give an apologetic for doing church more simply. Thom Rainer and Eric Geiger have already covered that ground.[3] My point is to explain that simplifying our programming fueled our volunteer leadership culture. Think about it: when your church is doing too many things, not only are your people overwhelmed and sometimes confused, but your pool of volunteer leaders is greatly diluted. The way to make progress as a church is to encourage your best leaders to fill your most critical roles. And if your church has dozens of competing ministries going at once, you may find yourself in an unenviable position. You might have a volunteer with the leadership capacity to spearhead your entire small group ministry, thereby fueling the discipleship movement in your church, who is unable to serve in that role because she is too busy coaching the church softball team. Now, I love softball as much as the next guy, but what a waste! Simplification allowed us to free up our best leaders and paved the way for them to have greater kingdom impact.

We began to get rid of committees and reduce competing programs. Those two decisions, along with an early working model of volunteer leadership in our youth ministry, laid the foundation for where we are today as a church. In fact, a half dozen or more of those original student leaders who led our youth ministry are currently on staff at Grace, still shaking up the way we do church and implementing the principles that helped shape that original ministry. But the big shift didn't come until we had a moment of clarity in 2011.

Sarah

Meet Sarah

Sarah's "real" job: Stay-at-home mom

Sarah's volunteer role: Preaching Team

How were you initially asked to volunteer in your high-capacity role? "I was leading our CORE (membership) class ministry, and we had just wrapped up our first new and improved eight-week class. Week 8 concluded with dinner at the home of one of our volunteer pastors, Jim. Pastor Derek was there as well. Jim and Derek did the final teaching, and I was acting as the class host. As we were saying goodbye to the class participants and helping Jim and Susan clean up, Derek casually dropped a bomb on me in the kitchen. . . . He said, 'I think you should preach a sermon sometime soon.' I had led a Life Group. I had taught classes. I had hosted our Sunday worship services. But preach? I felt simultaneously thrilled and sick to my stomach."

What is energizing about your high-capacity role on the preaching team? "I cannot deny that Jesus has both saved me from and to so much. To know that I, too, have gifts from the Holy Spirit and that others recognize and affirm those gifts is both encouraging and energizing. The one thing that compelled me to say yes and continues to compel me is the undeniable sense that while this is about what my pastor has asked me to do, it is more about what the Holy Spirit has called me to do."

What are some things that make you feel like you are a part of staff? "I am asked to be a full participant in staff meetings and in preaching team meetings. I have an annual review. I have to put together calendar and budget proposals for ministry teams I lead, and I am included in staff appreciation activities."

What advice would you give to other people who may be considering stepping into a high-capacity volunteer role? "Doing ministry seems to be less about a job position than it is about calling and gifting. God calls all kinds of people to all places in ministry, regardless of gender, age, prior experience, education, or life stage. He gifts us the same with no regard for our human or cultural notions of who would be best suited to do something. When He calls, listen, be brave, say yes!"

CHAPTER 3

A Moment of Clarity

Creativity and insight almost always involve an experience of acute pattern recognition: the eureka moment in which we perceive the interconnection between disparate concepts or ideas to reveal something new.

—Jason Silva

You're Not as Good as You Think You Are

My father-in-law, Chuck, is a freak of nature. He's seventy-eight years young, he's been a residential builder in the construction industry his whole life, and he knows a little of everything about everything. At seventy-eight, he still wakes up at 5:00 a.m. every day, drinks his black coffee, reads the newspaper, eats his breakfast, and does a few calisthenics. He then buttons up his Carhartt overalls and laces up his well-worn Redwing boots, and he's out the door by 7:00. He fixes tractors, renovates old barns, replaces his own shingles, mows acres of fields every day with his brush hog. The man refuses to slow down. However, like most of us, he might not be the best judge of some aspects of his own qualities.

A new TED-Ed video based on a lesson by psychologist David Dunning explains a phenomenon known as the Dunning-Kruger effect.[4] In short; the research suggests that we're not very good at evaluating ourselves accurately. We frequently overestimate our own abilities. It happens in the workplace, it happens in relationships, it even happens morally and spiritually.

In his book *The Curse of the Self*, Mark Leary references a survey by *U.S. News and World Report*. One thousand Americans were asked, "Who do you think is most likely to get into heaven?" Then-President Bill Clinton had a 52 percent chance. Then-superstar Michael Jordan came in at 65 percent, while Oprah Winfrey got a 66 percent. Mother Teresa had a whopping 79 percent of people who thought she was likely to go to heaven.

The most interesting part of the survey was that only one vote-getter topped Mother Teresa, getting almost 90 percent of votes. Do you know who it was? It was the person completing the survey.[5] Collectively respondents essentially said, "Out of all the other people in the world, Mother Teresa has the best chance of getting into heaven. But there is one person that has a better shot than her at getting in—and it's me!"

We humans have an almost limitless capacity for self-deception. We grossly overestimate our own goodness. We make ourselves heroes of our stories. We exaggerate our roles in victories and absolve ourselves of blame in failures. We think, "If my boss accepts my proposal, it's because I am smart, but if the proposal bombs, it's because of these terrible working conditions." Or, "If people like my sermon, it's because I'm such a great rhetorician, but if they don't, well it's their fault for having the mental capacity of a second-grader."

Back to my father-in-law. The whole family was gathered for a holiday meal when he made the big announcement. He had recently noticed that his other octogenarian friends were all starting to get shorter, and he became curious about his own height. So, he asked his old buddy to come for a visit to his tractor barn. Chuck handed the shrinking friend his trustiest tape measure and stood tall. The results of this very unofficial physical examination were staggering. Chuck reported proudly to the dinner table that he was, at the ripe old age of seventy-eight, getting taller! He must have hit a sort of late-in-life second puberty. In fact, he added that he had recently been to the eye doctor, and guess what? His eyesight was also getting better! At that point one of his daughters said, "Dad, that's two strikes, one more crazy claim from you and we're having you committed!" Don't tell him, but I question the accuracy of his findings.

There is another group of people who are highly prone to self-deception. I know them well because I am one of them. They are pastors. If my church is growing, it must be due to my brilliant preaching or my incredible leadership. If my church is stagnant, it must be the evils of our culture, or the secular part of the country where my church is located, or the spiritual attack that we're facing right now. Maybe these things are a form of self-deception. And maybe there is another way of thinking about the problems we face.

Pastoral Excuse-Making

I remember feeling like I was wearing blinders. I couldn't see clearly around the next corner. The church didn't seem to be thriving like we had hoped, and I was seeking respite in my go-to excuses. Year after year, as we evaluated our ministry, I seemed to conjure up some recurring reasons for our lack of progress.

The first excuse was always *staffing*. We didn't have the right paid staff, and we didn't have enough paid staff. Our small group ministry was stifled because we didn't have the money to hire a small group director. That new staff position always seemed like the priority that got squeezed out at the end of the budgeting process. We had a great idea for a community outreach program, but we didn't have a great candidate to lead it. I was personally passionate about community outreach, but my time was needed elsewhere. I told myself, "If we could just hire a few more key staff, our problems would be solved."

The second excuse centered around *geography*. Erie, Pennsylvania is a very difficult region of the country for evangelical churches. It is deeply Catholic, so most of the people are either devout Catholics or former Catholics. And the former Catholics always have a grandma who currently remains devout, and she would never approve of them attending a church like Grace! When it comes down to God or Grandma, they always seem to side with Grandma. In addition, Erie has long been a test market for new products because people here are so averse to change. The phrase "if it can work in Erie, it can work anywhere" has become a well-known mantra. In addition, Erie is one of the snowiest and cloudiest cities in the country. It can be "dreary Erie" on a lot of days, but when the sun shines, there's nowhere better. The boating and fishing and sunsets over the lake are magnificent. The problem is, when it's sunny on a Sunday, church is the last thing on everyone's mind. You can insert your geographical excuses here. I've hung out with enough pastors to know that we all have them!

There are plenty of other excuses we came up with. And all the excuses had formed a kind of mental fog around our decision making. I remember many church strategy sessions ending with me shrugging my shoulders and saying, "Erie is just a tough place to do ministry," or "we just don't have enough money to hire that new staff position."

Our moment of clarity came when we got some other voices in the room to help assess and analyze our ministry. Outside voices can guard us from self-deception. They also help to neutralize our excuse making. And in my case, those voices helped me to see what was really going on in our church.

What's Your Greatest Asset?

It was 2011, and I stood at a whiteboard in a room overlooking the beautiful Lake Chautauqua. Our leadership team was on our yearly two-day planning retreat. The lower level of this breathtaking summer home (a mansion really) belonging to a Christian couple had been generously converted into a high-end retreat center. It had become our team's go-to getaway spot for many years. A lot of our best ideas originated at this place. It was a kind of "holy ground" for us. In this particular session, we were working through our annual SWOT analysis. This exercise (discussed more in chapter 13) allows for a well-rounded assessment of the current state of things. It also involves many voices, which are necessary so I'm not deceived into thinking that the church's success rises and falls on my preaching or clever ideas.

I assumed my place at the whiteboard, and we began brainstorming. "What are our church's greatest Strengths, Weaknesses, Opportunities, and Threats?" Some great stuff came out, but when we finished the exercise, I remember feeling unsatisfied. We had done a lot of good analysis, but something was missing. I asked, "Are we sure that's everything?" Then a pregnant pause. Our list of strengths consisted of the usual suspects: we had made some good advances in our worship, our facilities were in good shape, preaching was solid, we had some good in-roads in blessing our community and dealing with social justice issues in our inner city. As I was looking up and down the list, one of my insightful colleagues blurted out, "What about our people? The people of our church, where do they land on the list?"

That's it! I'm sad to admit that until that moment, we had never found words to describe our greatest strength as a church—*it's our people, dummy!* I went back to the crowded whiteboard and managed to squeeze the words "our people" right under the "Strengths" heading. The people of our church were, and are, our greatest asset. I'd be willing to bet it's true of your church too. You may just not have the words for it yet.

Think about it. The people in your church are incredible. They have access to other people you'll never have access to. They occupy positions in companies that you'll never be in. They have contacts in other businesses and industries that you'll never have. They hang out with personal tribes who are interested in motorcycles, or bowling, or CrossFit, or craft beers, or book clubs that you'll never be invited to. They have neighbors you don't know and coworkers you'll never meet. They also have skills and talents and expertise that you'll never have. And if your people were truly equipped, empowered, and unleashed in leadership for God's kingdom, the reach of your church would expand exponentially. The redemptive potential of each local church is mind boggling. Our people are our greatest asset. This was the first of two *aha* moments that year.

Lessons from Ephesians 4

Ephesians 4:11–12 says,

And he gave the apostles, the prophets, the evangelists, the shepherds and teachers, to equip the saints for the work of ministry,
for building up the body of Christ, . . .

Much has been written about these two short verses. Some have empha-
sized the five-fold ministry model, which is the idea that this passage identifies five offices: apostles, prophets, evangelists, shepherds, and teachers.
They would suggest that these five offices must be fulfilled in order for
the church to function at its fullest potential. Alan Hirsch has championed
the APEST leadership model complete with an online assessment to see
which of the five offices you might be most inclined to fill.[6]

Other large evangelical churches tend to focus on the "equip the saints
for the work of ministry" part of this passage. They take the approach that
the specific breakdown of the five roles is not exactly the point. Instead, the
point is the idea that God gave a handful of leaders, usually the paid staff, to
the church. And the role of those staff leaders is not to *do* the work of ministry but to *equip* the people of the church to do the ministry. The paid staff
administers while each member *ministers* through her acts of service as a volunteer. This is the approach that our church has adopted over the years. But
there are two clarifying questions to ask as you consider the implications of
these verses. One of the questions may apply more to smaller church pastors
and the other to larger church pastors. To smaller church pastors who find
yourselves doing most of the work I would ask:

1. *Can a single pastor have all five functions and do all the equipping?*

   The truth is . . . no. This passage (among others) is a clear call to the
   plurality of leadership within the church. Even the most skilled lone-
   ranger pastor couldn't pull this off. And the way the passage is worded
   suggests that no pastor should even try to pull this off. The only way

to assure this well-rounded approach to ministry is to make sure the pastor is surrounded by other equipping leaders. Not just doers of ministry, but equippers of people. Lone-ranger pastoring was never God's plan for his church.

The second question may apply more to larger church pastors:

2. *Does the function of equipping only apply to paid staff?*

Again, the answer is no. Paying multiple staff people to lead within the church is a modern luxury that is largely unknown throughout church history (and even in the modern world other than the West). It's safe to say that when Paul wrote these words in Ephesians 4:11–12 to the church in Ephesus, the prophets and evangelists and shepherds and teachers that he was picturing in his mind were all volunteer leaders. Large churches might be able to read Ephesians 4 and set out to hire people to fulfill all these roles, but what about the huge percentage of churches in America who are not a large church? What about the 60 percent of churches with fewer than a hundred people? [7] There is no way that the vast majority of churches could accomplish the ministry of "equipping the saints" with paid staff. Which means that the church must pursue equippers from among the ranks of volunteers.

These questions remind us that for the church to achieve God's dream, we must explore the empowering of leaders outside our traditional paying structures.

A Second "Aha" Moment: The Y Factor

Motivated by our realization that our people are our greatest asset and armed with passages like Ephesians 4 that suggested we reexamine the structures of the church; our team came to another seminal moment.

We read an article by Bill Hybels, cofounder of Willow Creek Community Church, called "The Y Factor."[8] Hybels's pastoral career has since ended under a cloud of allegations concerning sexual improprieties;

however, some of his insights still have value to the church. In the article, Hybels outlines a formula that his staff worked through that resonated deeply with our leaders at the time. The big takeaway from the article was that most churches don't have the financial resources to meet the growing ministry opportunities all around them with paid staff. They need to come up with alternative strategies.

Essentially, in the article Hybels described drawing a graph. I stood at our own board and recreated this graph for our team. The first part of the graph was a line ascending from left to right at a forty-five-degree angle that he called ministry potential or spiritual opportunity. Never has the spiritual and ministry opportunity in the church been higher. Then he drew another line from left to right from the same starting point. This was the financial resource line or how many paid staff could be hired. It was not growing at the same rate as the opportunity line—in fact, it was flat. So, the ministry opportunities were growing, but the ability to hire staff to seize those opportunities was not. Can anyone relate?

He then described how someone stood up and added algebra to the board. They wrote "X + Y = Z," where Z was the desired end result, the growing line up and to the right. This line represents bearing much fruit, seizing all the ministry opportunities that present themselves. X was the flat line, the line that stood for the financial limitations of paying staff. The person who added the math then said that in order to get from X to Z, we need to add a variable. And the variable is Y, which stood for volunteers.

THE Y FACTOR

Z = MINISTRY POTENTIAL

Y = VOLUNTEER LEADERS

X = PAID STAFF

$$X + Y = Z$$

The truth is, in every church, there is much more

ministry opportunity than the paid staff can handle. Financial limitations will never allow the number of staff (X) to increase fast enough to meet all the new opportunities. The only option is to greatly increase the number of volunteers (Y).

This was our second "aha" moment. We took the formula in a slightly different direction than Willow Creek did. Their conclusion was that they needed to "double Y." They set out to double the number of volunteers to accomplish their many ministry opportunities.

Our conclusion was instead of adding volunteers, what if we created a whole new group of ministry positions called "Volunteer Staff"? We would go after some of the high-capacity leaders in our church who were currently not involved or involved in other volunteer positions, and we would ask them to consider taking on big roles with big responsibilities. Roles that we would normally provide a salary for, but we'd like them to do it for free!

It was intimidating to consider asking so much of volunteers—but thankfully, asking them wasn't the first step. We had to ask ourselves some questions first.

Chasing Our Ministry Potential

The first order of business was to ask some critical questions that we probably should have been asking on a regular basis anyway: What are the ministries we're not currently doing that God wants us to do? Which ministries are our most strategic growth engines? If a new pastor took over for me tomorrow, which ministries would he or she stop or start immediately?

We identified a number of ministries that needed our attention right away. We needed to fan the flames of ministries like small groups, discipleship classes, ServErie (our community service ministry), guest follow-up, and one of our worship services that had become stagnant and lacked creative direction. We determined that if we could add solid leadership to these ministries that weren't currently receiving enough of our attention, it would have a profound impact on the health and growth of our church.

Once we had collectively identified our most strategic ministry needs, our team gathered to brainstorm a list of our high-capacity leaders. We were looking for people who were solid Christians with good character and strong faith. But we also wanted each one to have a proven track record of leadership either inside or outside the church. It didn't matter how busy they were; we weren't going to say their no for them. We would present the vision for volunteer staff and the specific vision for their role—no soft selling—and see what happened. We paired each high-capacity leader with one of our strategic needs and had a recruitment conversation. There is more detail on the specifics of these asks in part 2 of this book, but suffice to say, even I was surprised by the success rate. Every person we asked to be in one of those original positions said yes!

We were scheduled to host a Global Leadership Summit event at our church later that summer, and so we invited those key recruits along with our existing paid staff to attend. That event acted as a catalyst for the other key changes that were to come.

Key Changes

Adding volunteers to our staff forced us to consider some key changes, all of which I will explore in section two of this book. Probably the one we felt the most was changing our staff meetings from daytime to evenings. We also needed to communicate these new roles to various teams and at some level to the whole congregation. We cobbled together some work-stations. We ordered business cards. We created email addresses and official name tags. We posted these new names on the website and weekly bulletin right alongside the rest of our staff.

We were blurring the lines between clergy and laity. We were challenging the modern American church idea about who is qualified to do ministry and who's not. It started shaking us up in a good way.

CHAPTER 4

Everyone Is a Priest

Two-Track System

If an ancient Israelite priest were to take the stage at one of our churches today, it would be a shocking sight. The linen tunic, the colorful ephod (outer robe), the breastplate containing the twelve precious stones, the turban with a gold plate on the forehead, the Urim and Thummim stones used to determine God's will. It would be an intimidating and impressive display of ritualistic attire. But a priest's special clothing was just the tip of the iceberg.

There was a vast array of ceremonies and regulations and special orders associated with the Jewish priesthood. All priests were sons of Aaron from the tribe of Levi. They were the only ones who could serve in the sanctuary making sacrifices, keeping the lamps lit, and presenting offerings. They served behind the veil in an area of the holy place where only they had access. The whole religious life of Israel was built on a two-track system. There were the priests, and then there was everyone else. The holy people and the ordinary people. If you were a priest, there were special places only you could go, special prayers only you could pray, special clothes only you could wear.

The Tabernacle, the place of worship, also mirrored this two-track system. A curtain hung between the Holy Place and the outer parts of the temple providing a physical barrier that highlighted the two-track system. There were multiple divisions among the priesthood, the tabernacle, and later, the temple. In Leviticus 10:10, we find out the purpose of this whole system. God says it's "So that you can distinguish between the holy and the common, between the unclean and the clean."

The two-track system served as an object lesson to remind the people that God is holy—that he's set apart and that the people's sin has separated them from his presence. A holy mediator was needed to reconcile God and his people.

Everyday Priests

When Jesus came, he became the ultimate holy mediator. He didn't do away with the priesthood—he actually gave it to everybody. He didn't shut it down, he expanded it out. He turned the two-track system into a one-track system. One of the main symbols of this change in the system happened at the moment of the crucifixion. The Bible tells us that the moment Jesus gave up his last breath, the curtain in the temple that divided the Holy of Holies (where only the high priest could enter once a year) from the rest of the temple and the outer courts (where everyone else could enter) was torn in two (Matthew 27:51; Mark 15:38; Luke 23:45). The tearing of the curtain is very significant in how we approach God and approach ministry.

The curtain was a visible physical barrier indicating that access to God was prohibited because of his holiness. And his holiness remains unchanged. But what changed is our access to him, which is no longer through any priestly mediator other than Jesus. The author of Hebrews expounds on this very clearly: "we have confidence to enter the holy places" (Hebrews 10:19), and this is accomplished by the blood of Jesus. This is the "new and living way" (Hebrews 10:20) by which believers have access to the presence of God. This, coupled with the priesthood of Christ (Hebrews 10:21), forms the basis of the author's exhortation to believers: draw near to God (Hebrews 10:22), hold unwaveringly to our confession of faith (Hebrews 10:23), stir one another up to love and good works (Hebrews 10:24), and continually meet together to encourage one another in the faith (Hebrews 10:25).

But the tearing of the curtain not only signifies the fact that ordinary people can now enter into the holy place and access the very presence of God, but it also indicates that holiness can now invade the ordinary! The functions that had previously only been reserved for priests could now be multiplied in the lives of all true believers. Peter's first epistle describes it this way:

> But you are a chosen race, *a royal priesthood*, a holy nation, a people for his own possession, that you may proclaim the excellencies of him who called you out of darkness into his marvelous light. (1 Peter 2:9, italics added)

Do you understand what Peter is saying here? Because of what Jesus did on the cross, now *everyone* is a priest. But just like in the old days, being a priest comes with responsibilities. First and foremost, priests must be devoted to service of God. But more than that, priests take on the function of making sacrifices to God. Only in our case, these sacrifices are no longer animals and crops, but they come in the form of our bodies (Romans 12:1), our praise (Hebrews 3:15), our acts of service (Hebrews 13:16), and our prayers (Revelation 8:3–4).

The clear dividing line between clergy and laity has been erased. We are all ministers. Paul says in 2 Corinthians 5:18,

> All this is from God, who through Christ reconciled us to himself and *gave us* the ministry of reconciliation. (Italics added.)

Who is "us"? It's all of us! Every Christian has been entrusted with the ministry of reconciliation. Not just pastors, not just missionaries, not just church staff, but *all of us*! I wonder how many people in our modern churches understand their role as priests of the new covenant. I wonder how many churches would take on a whole new identity if they began to embody the priesthood of all believers.

Martin Luther's Take

The idea of the priesthood of believers is as old as the Bible itself but experienced a renaissance during the Protestant Reformation. The words in 1 Peter 2:9 provided an important insight for the reformer Martin Luther. It is well known that Luther was primarily motivated by his desire to combat the corruption within the church's formal priesthood, the selling of indulgences, and other misuses of the church's power. But, as a by-product, a recommitment to the priesthood of all believers became one of the lasting course-corrections of the Protestant Reformation.

While Luther didn't use the exact phrase "priesthood of all believers," he pushed back against the medieval version of the two-track system. Christians shouldn't be divided into two classes, "spiritual" and "secular." Luther advanced the doctrine that all baptized Christians are priests in the sight of God regardless of their occupation. He said,

> That the pope or bishop anoints, makes tonsures, ordains, consecrates, or dresses differently from the laity, may make a hypocrite or an idolatrous oil-painted icon, but it in no way makes a Christian or spiritual human being. In fact, we are all consecrated priests through baptism . . . [9]

Luther never went so far as to suggest that there is not a role for formal clergy. But his perspective was that a designated member of the clergy is simply a person who is identified and elected by his fellow "priests" to fulfill the roles of the office:

> . . . none of us is born an apostle, preacher, teacher, pastor; but there all of us are born solely priests. Then we take some from among these born priest and call and elect them to these offices that they may discharge the duties of the office in the name of all of us. [10]

Luther's *Ninety-Five Theses* accomplished the Medieval equivalent of "going viral" thanks to the newly invented printing press. One year later,

Pope Leo X ruled that Luther's teachings were "scandalous and offensive to pious ears." He gave Luther 120 days to recant. Luther didn't do it. Even if he had recanted, the damage was already done. New ideas were spreading, and the growth and revival of Christianity was being carried along by nonordained, ordinary people. These were the high-capacity volunteers of the Middle Ages.

Luther's emphasis on the priesthood of all believers—along with other movements, reforms, and counter-reforms at that time—had an historic ripple effect of lay empowerment. New Bible translations, church-planting movements, and revivals were all being led by nonclergy. Think about the number of Christian hospitals, orphanages, schools of higher education, support groups, and missionary societies that were started by volunteers. Religious orders (nuns and monks who were not clergy) started social justice organizations that changed entire communities. The renewed emphasis on the priesthood of all believers changed the trajectory of Christ's work in the earth.

Finding Our Way Back

Yet, regrettably throughout history, the church has often drifted back into the two-track system. Many people have been conditioned to think that it's primarily the pastor's job to teach the Bible, visit the sick, counsel the broken, serve the poor, and evangelize the lost. However, a clergy-centric system will always end in disappointment because it's not God's plan for the New Testament church. Everyone is a priest. And because they are, if you are a pastor or leader in a local church, you must make it your number-one priority to multiply the priesthood within your congregation. Think about the momentum and revival that flowed out of the Protestant Reformation and other movements that followed. Maybe God will do it again through the unleashing of a whole new wave of mobilized Christians into important ministry endeavors.

It will be very difficult because most churchgoers gladly allow the pastor to do all the ministry. I have had people tell me, "That's what we pay *you* for" and, "This is *your* job, I have a real job." And many pastors have complied with the two-track system. They think, "I feel guilty asking volunteers to do something that they've clearly hired *me* to do." But we must push past these barriers and get back to God's vision for his church. Everyone is a priest.

Everyone deserves to experience the thrill of being used as an instrument in the hand of God. Many people don't necessarily find deep joy and spiritual meaning in their nine-to-five jobs. Many are simply putting food on the table without a sense of eternal satisfaction in their day-to-day work. But pastors and church leaders have been given the indescribable privilege of inviting people into the thrill of knowing that God himself has used them to touch a human life.

We can't apologize for inviting people into ministry in the church. They're our fellow priests, saved, sanctified, and commissioned to do the same ministry work we do. Pastor, if you try to do all the ministry yourself, you will rob people in your congregation of their eternal privileges as priests, and in the process, you will stifle the growth of your church.

CHAPTER 5

Imagine the Church Unleashed

What's Your 87 Percent?

The Founder, starring Michael Keaton, tells the true story of Ray Kroc, the man who took McDonald's from humble diner to global dominance. It's an incredible account of a man rising to power while also leaving some destruction in his wake. In the early days of McDonald's, the original founders, Maurice "Mac" and Richard "Dick," learned a key lesson about simplifying their menu around the bestselling products. They had to constantly fight (among both themselves and their franchisees) to keep their menu from becoming too diversified and confusing.

For many years, McDonald's fought off the tendency to try to do too much with their menu. I'm sure they continue to fight this. Just look at their attempt at the McPizza back in the 1980s! To see an example of their menu drift, look at this menu from 1943 that included barbecued beef, peanut butter and jelly with fries, ham and baked beans, tamales and chili, and a tempting item called the "Aristocratic Hamburger." Beverages included giant malts, ice cream sodas, floats, Coca-Cola, and coffee.

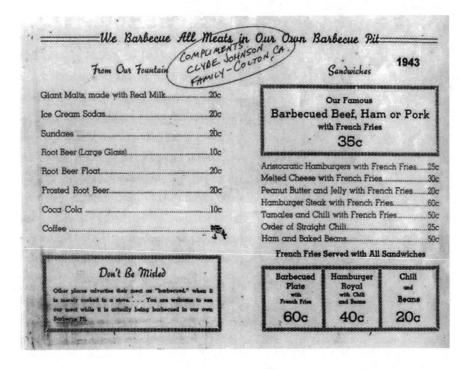

[A McDonald's menu from 1943 shows the wide selection on offer to early customers, and nothing costs more than 60 cents[11]]

Along the way, Ray Kroc became the heavy-handed enforcer of menu integrity. He urged each franchise to resist the temptation to offer everything to everyone and simply focus on what they did best: their core products. Each franchise needed to heed one of Mac McDonald's early business lessons. During his original analysis of their sales, Mac discovered that 87 percent of total sales could be attributed to three items: burgers, fries, and drinks. At the same time, huge amounts of stock and space and energy were being wasted on the other 13 percent: underdemanded items. By ruthlessly eliminating the less popular items on the menu, the business could focus on delivering their very best products efficiently and at top quality.

That old McDonald's menu with the barbecued beef, peanut butter and jelly sandwich, and tamales and chili could easily be the visual representation of the weekly calendar of most pastors. The menu is too full, and the options are way too many. Preaching, counseling, meetings, rehearsals, financial decisions, visitation, crisis management. It's too much.

I am part of a network of pastors in Pennsylvania that is spearheaded by LCBC Church in Lancaster, Pennsylvania under the leadership of Pastor David Ashcraft. During one of our sessions, we brainstormed the responsibilities of a lead pastor. We quickly came up with fourteen roles before the conversation was halted and we said, "OK, that's enough to start with!" Here's the list:

- Teacher
- Doctrine Protector
- Vision Caster
- Leader of Leaders
- Mouthpiece to the Community
- Model of Evangelism and Discipleship
- Fund Raiser
- Creator of Culture
- Congregational Coach
- Key Recruiter
- Gatekeeper against Mission Drift
- Protector of Church Unity and Identity
- Leadership Development Champion
- Networker with Other Leaders

We concluded that, amid the avalanche of expectations, the number-one responsibility of every pastor is simply the ability to focus on the right thing. Both organizational focus and personal focus is key. Ray Kroc would probably advise you to take a look at that confusing and disjointed menu that you call a job description and begin to figure out what is your

87 percent. What are those few areas that, when you focus time and energy on them, produce the greatest return for your church?

Find Your Cornerstone Calling

The act of pruning down your roles can be a ruthless process, but every leader must go through it. You need to ask and answer, "What is it that *only* I can do?" What are those core roles that God has specifically called me to do?" This process includes identifying your contributions that have the greatest impact on your church. This is your 87 percent. I like to call this your "cornerstone calling." When you boil down your job into its most basic functions—these are the things you simply can't give away. They are yours to own.

My cornerstone calling revolves around three things: 1) vision, 2) preaching, and 3) leading our leaders. Everything else that I find myself doing, I need to give away to high-capacity volunteers. I recognize that this list will be different for each pastor. Your list will be determined by your own gifts and skills, the size of your church or organization, and the makeup of the team around you. But these three things make up my cornerstone calling.

1. **Vision:** This means I am regularly creating and communicating a compelling vision and then making sure we stay on track to accomplish the outcomes that flow from it. We typically operate in three- to five-year vision cycles at Grace. It usually involves focusing on several key initiatives during that time frame, defining specific outcomes to be achieved, creating wording and storylines around each of the outcomes along with communication tools like brochures and websites, and then raising money around those vision initiatives.

2. **Preaching:** This involves leading our team of preachers, which currently includes six members, determining our sermon series calendar for the year, assuring that all sermons are well prepared

and biblically based, creating and/or reviewing all sermon outlines before they are sent to our creative team, and evaluating sermons after the fact.

3. **Leading our leaders:** This involves creating leadership content for our full staff, running point in our top leadership teams in the church (our lead team and our elder team), creating training modules for other levels of leadership within our church such as life group leaders, ministry leaders, and community leaders.

The most difficult task by far is to clear away all the clutter. And if we're not extremely careful as pastors, we'll find ourselves like McDonald's, serving tamales and peanut butter and jelly sandwiches when we should be sticking to burgers and fries. Churches deserve leaders who are delivering high-quality ministry in an efficient, God-honoring way. What is your cornerstone calling? Figure it out, write it down, and then give away everything else.

Acts 6: From Overwhelmed to Unstoppable

At the very beginning of the church, the apostles discovered their 87 percent and made the necessary adjustments. In Acts 6, the apostles reached a moment in their ministry that is all too familiar to most ministry leaders; they realized that there was not enough time or resources to do all the ministry that God had called them to do. So, what did they do? Did they burn the midnight oil and wear themselves out trying to do it all themselves? Did they wring their hands and complain at the apostle-training seminars that they didn't have enough money to hire staff? Did they whine about how difficult ministry was in their part of the ancient Middle East? No.

They identified their cornerstone calling and then gave everything else away to high-capacity volunteers.

Greek-speaking widows had complained that there was favoritism being shown at the church's food pantry ministry. This was a potentially sticky situation. There was a low-key accusation of racism going on here.

The Greek widows said that the Jewish widows were being given special treatment by the Jewish ministry leaders and the Greeks were being
neglected.

So, the apostles gathered the church together and made a stunning
declaration. They said, "It is not right . . . that we should serve tables." How
dare they! How unspiritual! You mean these godly men had better things
to do than to serve the poor and the needy? They didn't even say it's not
"convenient," or it's not "efficient"—they said it's not "*right*." I dare you to
try a little experiment. Just throw a quick post up on to social media suggesting that you don't think it's right for you to serve those in need. Let
me know how it works out.

Pastors, when a member of your congregation insists that it has to be
you who visits, or *you* who preaches each week, or *you* who counsels; if it
falls outside your cornerstone calling, it's not *right* for you to keep doing
that. The apostles decided that they needed to focus on what only they
could do, which was praying and preaching. Look at the text in Acts 6:2–4:

> *It is not right* that we should give up preaching the word of God to
> serve tables. Therefore, brothers, pick out from among you seven
> men of good repute, full of the Spirit and of wisdom, whom we
> will appoint to this duty. But we will devote ourselves to prayer
> and to the ministry of the word. (Emphasis added.)

They said no to what was good so they could say yes to what was best.
And to continue to expand their ministry, they decided to find not just
volunteers but volunteer *leaders* who would supplement the apostles' leadership with practical ministry. Notice the qualifications of the seven volunteer leaders. They were filled with the Spirit, they were full of faith, and
judging by their names, they were of Greek descent. In other words, they
were able to reach people that the Jewish apostles were unable to reach.
But they needed to be empowered and authorized to do so. In verse 6, we
see the apostles unleashing them for this new role as the apostles "prayed
and laid their hands on them."

The apostles knew that in order for this new Christian movement to reach its full potential, they needed to stay crystal clear on their cornerstone calling. But instead of ignoring other ministry opportunities and instead of waiting to "hire more staff," they decided to solve it with high-capacity volunteers. This approach gave the apostles, as it can give you, three opportunities that they wouldn't have had otherwise:

1. It allowed them to reach people they were not positioned to reach.
2. It allowed them to address pressing ministry needs right in front of them.
3. It allowed them to focus on what only they could do.

And we can see the result in Acts 6:7:

> And the word of God continued to increase, and the number of the disciples multiplied greatly in Jerusalem.

What started with the apostles feeling overwhelmed turned into an unstoppable movement. What was the key? Giving away ministry to the right leaders and letting them run. $X + Y = Z$. As they gave ministry away to the nonclergy of the day, the redemptive potential of the church started to be actualized.

Fulton Street Revival

We see a more recent example of nonclergy ministry impact in nineteenth-century America. The year was 1857, and business was booming in the United States. So was the population. The country was feeling the positive effects of the Industrial Revolution that led to material prosperity for many. But as greed was on the rise, the overall spiritual climate of the country was declining.[12]

The population growth in New York City consisted mainly of working-class laborers who were largely unchurched. Addictions like alcoholism were on the rise, and hot topics like slavery were dividing the nation. What would God do to address the needs of a divided nation? He raised up a high-capacity volunteer. A businessman named Jeremiah Lanphier who was deeply committed to prayer.

Shortly before noon on Wednesday, September 23, 1857, Lanphier opened the doors of an average-looking room in the consistory building on Fulton Street in the financial district of Manhattan for a noon prayer meeting. No one came until around 12:30.[13] That first day, a total of six people showed up. But those six people represented five different church denominations, and all were simply there to pray. The next week there were fourteen, and the following week there were around thirty. There were no discussions, only praying and singing. Soon it was determined that weekly meetings were not enough, so they began to gather daily. Within weeks, there were thousands of business leaders and workers meeting every day in prayer. The gatherings began to spread to other cities. People were being converted to Christ, at times ten thousand people a week in New York City alone. The revival spread like wildfire across the country. It is estimated that nearly one million people were converted out of a national population of thirty-five million. This outpouring is known as the Fulton Street Revival of 1857, and it may have been the greatest awakening ever experienced by the United States of America.

Why did this happen? Because a group of pastors figured out a slick new strategy? No. Because a well-funded missionary hit the streets? No again. But because a businessman (not a clergyman) with a vision started a noon-time prayer meeting. The Fulton Street revival was born on the prayers of businessmen and women, a new class of priests, who were crying out to God.

Acts 6:7 could be applied to America in 1857 and the decades to follow: "And the word of God continued to increase, and the number of the disciples multiplied greatly in [Manhattan and beyond]."

Everybody Is Bivocational

Bivocational ministry for pastors is an old concept that's experiencing new life in recent years. Bivocational just means someone who works both as the pastor of a local church as well as in the secular marketplace simultaneously. The church might provide a portion of the pastor's salary, but the rest comes from a second profession. Daniel Im, the coauthor of *Planting Missional Churches*, suggests that a bivocational approach should be a first option for church planters and not a last resort.[14] And, in many cases, the mission of the church itself calls for the pastor to be bivocational from both a funding and a networking perspective. Ed Stetzer suggests that being bivocational is not a penalty but an opportunity for pastors. He notes that already more than one-third of American pastors are bivocational and this number will probably grow. In other countries, the percentage is certainly much higher.[15]

But what if the concept of bivocational ministries wasn't just applied to pastors but to entire congregations? Certainly not every individual would need to carry the full weight of pastoral leadership in addition to their paying jobs, but a mindset shift could be greatly beneficial. Someone could be a bivocational public high school teacher and small group leader, or an insurance agent and nursery coordinator, or maybe a tool and die maker and guest experience team supervisor.

We have found that many of the leadership skills people learn at work can be applied to ministry, and the skills learned in ministry can be helpful at work. This mindset shift can also lead to increased invitations. Just like the kids in the old youth ministry days, our adult volunteer leaders are more apt to invite unchurched coworkers to a ministry that they've taken ownership in. Their posture has shifted from being a consumer of goods and services to being a part-owner in the company. And as a result, we have found that our high-capacity volunteers carry a contagious authenticity that flows into their circles of influence.

There are plenty of biblical examples of bivocational ministry. Paul was a tentmaker and leather worker. He obviously hung onto this trade so that he could "work with his hands and be dependent on no one" (1 Thessalonians 4:10–12). He also wrote to the church that "we worked night and day so that we might not burden any of you while we proclaimed to you the gospel of God" (2:1). So much for healthy boundaries! But Paul also did not discourage paid ministry responsibilities. In fact, in 1 Corinthians 9, he makes a strong case for the ministers to receive a wage worthy of their work.

It seems that Paul himself, along with some of the other apostles (especially the fishermen), kept an active trade at the ready throughout their ministry. But let's think one level down from the apostles for a moment. Call to mind the impact that was made for the gospel by bivocational volunteer leaders. There is strong biblical support for the idea that the gospel traveled to more new locations on the wings of business leaders than it did even by the apostles.[16] Luke seems to go out of his way to point out that it was laypeople, not the apostles, who were leading in the spread of the gospel in the book of Acts. The longest sermon recorded in the New Testament was delivered by Stephen—a volunteer deacon in the church of Jerusalem. Lydia in Thyatira was a house church leader, but also the leader of her guild. In *History of Christian Missions*, Stephen Neill says that none of the great Christian centers were established by the twelve apostles. The churches at Alexandria, Antioch, and even Rome were inaugurated by marketplace leaders who were also leading ministries.[17]

A true Acts 6 unleashing of the church will only happen when high-capacity lay leaders are unshackled from church busywork and freed to lead to their full potential.

Seven Channels for Changing the World

The problem is, most people sitting in the pews of most churches don't realize that the skills and gifts that they've developed throughout their lifetime could be used in ministry. They also don't recognize that their relational influence has amazing gospel potential.

In chapter 7 of his compelling book *Next Christians*, Gabe Lyons provides a helpful look at the seven channels of cultural influence. He points out that whole cultures are shaped when networks of leaders, representing the different social institutions of a culture, work together toward a common goal. Then he goes on to identify the seven social institutions that govern any society:

Business

Government

Media

Church

Arts and Entertainment

Education

The Social Sector

The combined output of ideas from these seven channels hold the power to drive an entire nation. He suggests that if even just a few influencers from each of these seven channels work together toward a common goal, it requires relatively little time and energy to bring meaningful change to an entire culture.[18]

There is one conclusion to Lyons's findings that continues to captivate my imagination. This conclusion positions the church at an incredible advantage when it comes to shaping culture. He points out that the church is the only one of these seven channels of influence that convenes members of the other six every week all in one place. Think of the potential! The reality is that many of those people from each sector still think that the highest and best use of their training and education is their role in that sector—their "real job." But what if we could inspire them? What if we could unleash them? What if we could remind them that their skills and influence could be used for kingdom purposes? If the church could inspire the leaders of various sectors to work together and pool their brainpower for kingdom endeavors, we could see whole communities change.

Meet Jim

Jim's "real" job: CPA Partner

Jim's volunteer role: Pastor of Staff Care

How were you asked to serve in a high-capacity volunteer role? "I was unable to balance some new challenges at my 'real job' and asked for a month off. This allowed for some changes which

Jim ultimately opened doors for me to serve at the church. The vision for my role, which was a new position, was presented to me by one of the Grace staff members. I was then given the opportunity and responsibility to develop a job description and establish some goals for the new role. Eventually, I was invited to join lead team on an interim basis. The invitation was made at the first [day] of a two-day retreat that was delayed until after tax season so that I could participate."

What energizes you about your volunteer role? "Listening to staff concerns and challenges and helping them walk through a Christ-centered resolution brings me a lot of joy. I am also energized by helping our staff to discern the different reasons certain things may not make sense to them, and then encouraging them to move forward. I also love helping marriages to thrive. Part of my job is to be a sounding board for ideas and a resource to address concerns. In those moments I get to rely on God for answers, because I usually have no specific experience to draw from. But being used by God in those situations is incredibly fulfilling."

What are some challenges you have faced? "Trying to stay connected to staff needs and regularly praying about them is challenging because I also have another full-time job to attend to. It can also be intimidating working with pastors that are way more gifted than I am in most areas of ministry."

How were you made to feel part of the staff? "I have been included in many critical conversations and was consistently asked for my input. I have had a seat at many tables, and having the chance to be a part of the decision-making process for the entire church makes me feel like my voice is important. I have also been given the freedom to make key decisions and have even supervised paid staff. I am held accountable for time away and other responsibilities that would normally be reserved only for people who are paid."

What would you say to others who might be considering a high-capacity volunteer role at their church? "It will change your life for the better. It will add value and meaning to your 'real' job. It will help you stay close to Christ and will add purpose and joy to your time on earth. I would also challenge you to be prepared to make significant changes in your lifestyle and routines. I have found it very important to find an accountability partner, a mentor, and a mentee. They will help you stay grounded and focused on your relationship with Christ and your marriage."

Six Barriers for Pastors

"A challenge only becomes an obstacle when you bow to it."

—Ray Davis

Establishing a volunteer leadership culture isn't easy. And the first step is often the hardest step. I've noticed six barriers in particular that can keep pastors feeling stuck. These barriers will hold you back from recruiting and empowering leaders who could take your ministry to the next level.

The ENERGY Barrier—"I'm barely surviving as it is."

Being a pastor is hard. On a recent Sunday morning, all the following interactions happened to me within the first twenty minutes following a worship service: As soon as the service ended, the whole worship team came off the stage to give me high-fives for an "amazing" message. I'm certain their encouragement was related to the fact that my final point was about the importance of worship! My hand was still tingling from the final high-fives when a member of the congregation pulled me aside due to concerns over the theology in point #2 of my message. He felt that God had been telling him to call me out for my "false teaching" for some time now, and today was the last straw. I nodded and moved on so that I could get to my office and grab a much-needed bottle of water. On the way a middle-aged mom who had just sent her first daughter off to college needed advice. Her daughter had just informed her that she was planning to have sex with another girl. She asked, "Pastor, I'm going to talk to her on the phone this afternoon, what advice should I give her?" Uhhhhh . . . I quickly shared a few thoughts that came to mind—but I still needed some water with the next service quickly approaching. So, I pulled away only to bump into a young man sobbing uncontrollably. He had just lost his mother suddenly in a tragic accident. Could we go to the prayer room to pray? Of course. Yes, of course! This is what it's all about. Needless to say, I preached the next sermon parched.

Being a pastor is hard. And my version of pastoring is a piece of cake compared to those who lead small churches. In the same twenty minutes that I just described, smaller church pastors could probably add mopping up a coffee spill in the fellowship hall, trying to remove some screeching feedback at the soundboard, scrambling to find a fill-in for the no-show in the nursery, and slowing down the junior high kid who just ran by in the hallway like Dash from *The Incredibles*. And pastoring might only be their part-time gig! That pastor probably has to go home and get ready for a "real job" on Monday morning.

"Who in the world has time to recruit and develop high-capacity volunteer leaders?" you may be thinking. "I'm barely surviving as it is." And so, in many cases, the plan is to just keep working and working until one day hopefully you'll have enough money to pay for that new staff person who will take some of these responsibilities off your shoulders. You conclude, "Right now, I'm just too busy with ministry to worry about this volunteer leader thing."

Well, that's exactly the point, isn't it? Maybe the reason that the church isn't growing enough to hire that new staff person is because you are spread too thin. You're doing a lot of things, but they may not be the things you need to be doing to actually disciple your congregation and grow the impact of your church.

Many churches, big and small, get caught in this catch-22. It's a never-ending cycle of waiting until they hire the next staff position, but never quite growing to the place where they can afford to hire that person. The two greatest tools at every leader's disposal are time and energy. So you must constantly ask yourself where you will spend your time and where you will focus your energy. I would think that most leaders would want to leverage their time and energy on those tasks that will bring the greatest return. Work on those areas that will multiply ministry and will have the greatest kingdom impact.

The truth is you have to *spend* time to *save* time. And the investment of time up front on recruiting and building and empowering volunteer leaders will bring a return on investment that will build God's kingdom and your church in incredible ways. The first decision is the hardest of all: saying no to a bunch of good things so that you can say yes to the things that will have the greatest impact on your church. I believe one of those most important things is empowering high-capacity volunteer leaders to take on significant ministry roles. Yes, it's hard, but the payoff is worth it.

The OBLIVION Barrier: "I didn't know it was an option."

Some pastors legitimately have never considered the possibility of inviting volunteers from their church to step into staff-level leadership roles. Maybe denominational biases, theological frameworks, or just church traditions didn't allow you to go there. You were oblivious to the possibility. I pray that this book is a wakeup call for you.

Sometimes we're bound by limits that don't actually exist. I was in a leadership workshop one time where the presenter was discussing overcoming the limits that we place on ourselves. To illustrate his point, the presenter asked for a couple of volunteers. He was going to conduct a makeshift standing long jump competition. The volunteers from the audience thought they were going to be competing against each other, but there was a surprise in store. The presenter lined up the jumpers and one at a time he told them to simply jump as far as they possibly could. He gave everyone a chance to limber up and stretch out. "You're only going to get one chance at this, so do your absolute best possible jump on the first try."

By this time, the jumpers were highly motivated, and one at a time they took their turn at the line. The presenter carefully measured each jump, putting the person's initials on a chalk line where they landed. After the first round of jumps, the furthest jumper was looking for his first-place prize, but the competition wasn't over. The presenter asked everyone if they had given their best effort. They assured him they had. Had everyone accomplished their maximum length under the current condition? Yes, no question they had.

At this point the presenter confessed to telling a white lie. They would, in fact, get a second chance to jump. But they had never been competing against each other—only against themselves. The only goal of the game was to jump further on the second jump than they had jumped on the first. He had a simple instruction: "Take your first distance, and just jump a little further." Guess what? They all jumped further. Every. Single. Person. Even though they had given maximum effort on the first jump.

It was a reminder that we are often bound by limits that don't exist. Roger Bannister conquered the four-minute mile in 1954. For the previous sixty years, runners had been trying to break that mark. Many scientists and medical experts concluded that it was physically impossible for the human body to go that pace over that distance. But once Bannister broke the mark, he showed that it was an option. Just forty-six days later, John Landy broke the barrier again. Then, just a year later, three runners broke the four-minute barrier in a single race. Since then, more than a thousand runners have conquered a barrier that had once been considered hopelessly out of reach.

I'm here to tell you that if you're a pastor who never knew this was an option . . . it is. Volunteer staff members are something you must consider. Refuse to be bound by limits that don't exist.

The CONSUMER Barrier: "They expect me to do everything."

The feedback I've gotten from pastors who try to implement this model from scratch has had a similar ring to it. People respond with comments like, "what do you think we are paying you for?" or "what kind of pastor do you think you are if you don't think _____ is part of your job description?" You can fill in the blank with all the usuals: hospital visitation, teaching Sunday school, leading the youth ministry, ordering the communion supplies, counseling troubled teenagers, volunteering at the local shelter. Each church, and each individual, has her own pet projects and ideas.

This mentality is a product of the consumeristic American church. It involves a mindset that says, "As far back as I can remember, the pastor *always* did these things." But just because someone thinks that doesn't mean it is biblical. Jesus never designed the church so that one hired hand was doing all the ministry and everyone else was critiquing it and then throwing a few bucks in the plate if they approve so that you can do it all again next week.

Pastors can either wring their hands and complain about consumerism in the church as if we're victims, or we can lead our churches into a better way—a more fulfilling way. Not just for the pastor but for everyone. When Paul describes the church as a body in 1 Corinthians, he doesn't assume the pastor (or anyone else) is going to function as the head, heart, hands, feet, mouth, and eyes, while the rest of the people are just ears and rears. Can you imagine how ridiculous a body like that would look—heavy on the ears and rears and light on every other part? That body would be sick, dysfunctional, and dying (and strangely fascinating to see just once).

Pastors must overcome the consumer barrier and lead our churches into a proper biblical view of the body of Christ—one where each body part is doing its job. There are only two ways I know of to shake your church out of a consumeristic slumber: *teach* them and *invite* them. One of my college professors suggested that ecclesiology (study of the church) is the most underdeveloped aspect of theology in the modern church. We need to first do a better job of *teaching* our churches what it means to be the true body of Christ with each member playing its part. Then we also need to boldly *invite* people to serve in important leadership roles within the church.

The QUALITY Barrier: "I don't have any high-caliber volunteers."

Some pastors look across the landscape of their congregation and don't see any obvious candidates for a high-capacity role in the church. They say things like "Everyone in my congregation is too old." Or "Everyone in my congregation is too spiritually immature."

These sweeping statements fail to acknowledge one basic truth, God knows how to make churches. He brings the right people to the right place at the right time. He doesn't expect you to do the job alone. Everyone is a priest. Usually when pastors come up against the QUALITY barrier, it means one of three things:

1. **You haven't gotten curious enough**. When you spend time with people, listening to their personal history, life experiences, and things they've accomplished along the way, your mind will be blown by the caliber and capacity of the most unexpected people. Think about it: the vast majority of adults in your church either are or were gainfully employed. That means that a business or organization paid them money to do actual work. And some of those people in your congregation weren't just workers; they were very good workers. Some of those people weren't just very good workers; they were leaders of other workers. Many of them are making a mark on the world through their job, and they could be making a mark in your church. Get to know them. Find out what makes them tick. Listen for cues about what lights them up and what they excel at. Then connect the dots to how God might use them. Become curious about the possibilities.

2. **You haven't gotten creative enough.** Sometimes pastors who say they don't have high-caliber people have pigeon-holed the role that they need filled. They have predecided: "The only position that would be helpful for me is a youth pastor. Or a counselor. Or a worship leader. And there is no one in my church who

is skilled at that thing, so this doesn't work for me." Instead, get creative and discover what *other* skills and capacities already exist in your congregation. Maybe you don't have a youth pastor but instead a sermon researcher, or a scheduling assistant: people who might give you fifteen to twenty hours per week in an area you didn't expect that would in turn create space for you to step into one of the roles you were trying to hire.

3. **You haven't developed people enough**. Sometimes pastors won't let a volunteer serve in a high-capacity role until they can do the job 100 percent as well as the pastor could do it. That probably either won't happen or will take too long for everyone involved. In his leadership podcast, Craig Groeschel proposes the 80 percent rule. That is, if someone can do something 80 percent as well as you, then give it to them. He suggests that he would take that number down to 50–60 percent if the person has momentum and potential. Give it to them and let them grow into it. Because, with some momentum, they might start at 60 percent but end up able to do the job 110 percent as well as you.[19] But this takes a developmental mindset. Most prefer a microwave method of leadership development, but this is more of a Crock-Pot approach. Think about when Jesus sent his disciples out two by two. According to our ministry sensibilities, he released them way too soon! They weren't ready. They were more of a "50 percent with potential" gamble. But Jesus was committed to developing them. He knew that when they returned, he would check in with them and coach them, and this would all be part of the developmental process.

So instead of succumbing to the notion that you don't have any high-caliber volunteers in your church, make sure that you're open to getting curious, being creative, and taking a chance on developing someone who might not seem quite ready yet.

The CONTROL Barrier: "No volunteer can do it like I do it."

It's easy to see why Moses was trying to hold on to control of the Israelites during the wilderness wanderings. He was the one who had received the barefoot calling from God at the burning bush. He was the one who had seen his staff become a snake. He was the one who made his own emancipation proclamation before Pharaoh demanding his people's release from slavery. He was the one who called down the plagues, and followed the pillar of fire, and parted the sea, and brought water from a rock, and called down room service for a million people from heaven in the form of manna. He was the one leading everybody to the promised land. He was the man of God, the anointed one, the direct line with the Father. God had determined that Moses was the man, so in the wilderness all the decisions needed to flow through him. That's the way it had always been.

Which makes the rebuke of Exodus 18 all the more startling. Moses' father-in-law, Jethro, sits him down for a little talk. I've had some heart-to-heart talks with my father-in-law, and they can be unnerving . . . they can also be pretty direct. Whether old Jethro's advice was motivated out of concern for his daughter and grandkids or his love of God's people doesn't really matter. He gives Moses an enduring word that all of us can learn from in Exodus 18:17–18:

> Moses' father-in-law said to him, "What you are doing is not good. You and the people with you will certainly wear yourselves out, for the thing is too heavy for you. You are not able to do it alone."

As a result of this sage advice, Moses decided to decentralize his leadership. He realized he was trying to do the work of a hundred people instead of trying to find a hundred people to do the work. So he gave responsibility away by dividing people into thousands, and hundreds, and fifties, and tens, and each group had a leader. These leaders acted as decision makers. The hard cases were brought to Moses, but the smaller matters they decided themselves. Moses had unknowingly become a bottleneck because he was trying to maintain control. Remember, the bottleneck is always at the top of a bottle. Which means the leader is usually the one slowing down the effectiveness of an organization if she insists on maintaining control.

Some of you "super-pastors" need to hear this today: "What you are doing is not good! It is too heavy for you." Too many pastors are control freaks. Whether it's a case of the messiah complex complete with a well-intentioned desire to help everyone, or it's a more sinister dose of narcissism that has been allowed to run unchecked for too long in your life; the inability to empower other leaders will eventually destroy you. Take it from Jethro.

We must never allow our pride to get in the way of God's kingdom. As I have found dozens of times now, while I may not think a volunteer could do it as good as me at the beginning, in the end, they do the job much better than I ever could. It's a humbling reminder that the body of Christ is a much better idea than a one man show.

The ROLE Barrier: "I can't ask a volunteer to do that."

The final barrier that most pastors face is the barrier of role. This usually takes one of three forms:

1. *That role seems Too Big for a volunteer.*

   Maybe you're still struggling to get your mind around the fact that someone would be willing to donate twenty to thirty hours per week to the church without pay. I remember our leadership team wrestling through the idea of asking Jim to be the site pastor at our largest location. At the time, Grace McKean was a congregation of about nine hundred people each weekend. Could we really ask someone to *volunteer* to lead a site of nine hundred people? It would involve leading a staff, coordinating care, speaking into discipleship, making sure kids and youth ministry were humming, participating in all the meetings that go along with being the leader at our largest site. Because of God's leading, and our strong central support system, we decided to ask Jim to consider this role. It would probably mean at least thirty hours per week as long as he was empowering others properly. To our surprise, he accepted the challenge!

I will never forget the surreal moment when I walked in to observe one of his staff meetings. There were about twenty people there. Every person in that room (except one part-time worship leader) was unpaid. What a team! Eventually, as that site continued to grow, we did bring in a paid site pastor, and Jim was promoted to a different leadership position. But in that moment, I realized once and for all that no role is *too big* for a volunteer.

2. *That role seems Too Important for a volunteer.*

As I stood up one Sunday morning for the opening announcements, I picked them out of the crowd in an instant. They were a brand-new family. Their formal attire gave them away. The suit on him and dresses on her and the girls in our come-as-you-are culture were a clear give-away. I made a beeline to greet Cleve and Diane after the service, and they were friendly enough. They invited me to visit their home and when I stopped by—they had a major concern. We had a young person in a T-shirt helping to serve communion that day. And serving communion was *too important* for just any old teenager to be doing. I was able to explain our philosophy on empowering volunteers and our emphasis on everyone having a role in the body of Christ. Not only did they come back, but soon Diane was serving as a high-capacity volunteer and eventually served on our preaching team! I'm sure early on that would have been a no-no because preaching was also *too important* for just anyone. But Diane found her voice!

There are a variety of roles in the church that seem at first to be too important for a volunteer to do. I would urge you to challenge your assumptions. Obviously, no matter what, churches should operate with proper controls and accountability for important functions. But I'm convinced that volunteers can be just as accountable as paid staff members and can be held to the same standard of performance. In fact, there are volunteer leaders who can probably do important jobs far better than some paid staff people! For years, we paid part-time financial administrators to help keep the church's books. And we did it in the name of proper control and accountability. Then we met Bernie, one of our long-standing high-capacity volunteers. He was a recently retired business manager with fantastic financial skills. He offered far more expertise than anyone we could afford to pay part time, and he did it as an act of service to God. Bernie has been on our staff now for nearly twenty years and has never taken a paycheck.

3. *That role seems Too Pastoral for a volunteer.*

There are some roles in the church that only the pastor has ever done. The word "pastor" isn't frequently used in the Bible. Instead, it originates from a Latin word for "shepherd." It is usually associated with the spiritual leader or shepherd of a local church. In 1 Timothy 3:1–7 and Titus 1:5–9, the words bishop, elder, and overseer are used interchangeably. The idea of an ordained pastor complete with seminary degree, denominational stamp of approval, ordination credentials, and certificates in Greek and Hebrew, is a fairly modern notion. For much of history, and still in many parts of the world, local church leadership has been determined by who is gifted and who is mutually agreed upon by the congregation.

I understand that different traditions have different views on the subject of what a pastor can and must do. But I would encourage you to push the envelope where you can. Even the Roman Catholic Church, which historically had very strict rules about the priest's role in the Mass, has loosened their restrictions due to the shortage of priests. Now lay deacons can be involved in a variety of ways that were once reserved for the priest alone. So, if in your tradition only the pastor can preach, raise up a gifted preacher from your congregation and give them a shot. Send the message that no role is *too pastoral* for a volunteer. If only the pastor can serve communion, or baptize, or visit people in the hospital, begin to let other respected members of the congregation get involved. Sure, you'll have some complaints, but you'll be surprised how empowered the rest of the congregation will feel.

Meet Bernie

Bernie

Bernie's "real" job: Currently retired but worked for Lord Corporation Aerospace Products. Bernie held positions in engineering, marketing and sales, quality, and plant management.

Bernie's volunteer role: Roles in financial management, operations, and special projects

How did you find your way into volunteer ministry? "In the year 2000, I was sixty-three years old in my forty-first year of working at Lord Aerospace Products in Erie. I had no intentions of retiring any time soon, but I was tiring of working 'for profit.' I wanted to work for the Lord. My wife and I had been attending Grace Church for two years. One day the Lord spoke to me, saying I should retire to spend time with my wife and to volunteer at Grace. I did so on my sixty-fourth birthday in 2001 and offered my services to Grace Church. I started off by visiting hospitals, but soon I was moved to a role with finances, then operations, and now special projects."

What have you enjoyed about being one of Grace's first volunteer staff? "It was honoring to be considered for such important roles in the church. It fulfilled my calling as I was working for the *Lord* and not Lord Corporation (despite having loved my forty-two years there). The challenges as the church grew in size were energizing for me. I was heavily involved in the sale of our former property, the construction and move into our new facility, and the addition of other multisite locations."

How were you made to feel part of the staff? "I started by working on-site two days a week, and gradually moved to full time. I definitely felt that I was part of staff as I interacted with the team on a daily basis. I was even honored to serve on the management team and then the lead team for seasons. While these roles were challenging and ventured into new areas for me, the Holy Spirit provided wisdom and direction. Not having to be paid was a real blessing for both me and the church."

What would you say to others who might be considering a high-capacity volunteer role at their church? "My coming to volunteer was a different path than for many who still must balance an outside job with church responsibilities. But I believe the Holy Spirit will speak in a way that makes the choice an easy one. I must say that there is no better job than working for the Lord at Grace Church, no matter what the role. The opportunity to be part of what God is doing through our church is special."

CHAPTER 7

Benefits of Making the Switch

My heart was full at our recent full church staff meeting. Two-thirds of the people there were not paid. And I saw among them a college football coach, a high school principal, a third-shift social worker, an advertising executive, a hospital administrator, an insurance agent, and on and on I could go. Each one finding purposeful ministry opportunities on our staff. I reflected on how fulfilling this approach to church has been, and how beneficial it has been to pursue a "different kind of church."

As I close out this first section of the book, I want to bring you in on what I see to be the top eight benefits of giving away ministry at a sometimes surprising rate to people who don't take a paycheck from the church. If any of you have been reading along and secretly thinking, "This sounds like a lot of work, I wonder what's in it for me?"—here's your answer.

Fulfill God's Dream for the Church

As you may have noticed already, I have my suspicions that the contemporary American church has, at best, drifted from God's original dream for his church. At worst, we've missed the mark entirely. When you read the New Testament book of Acts and the Pastoral Epistles, it doesn't take long before you realize that God's dream for his church doesn't seem to include a vision that a paid professional would do the ministry from buildings while crowds gather in person or online to spectate and give just enough money to fund the pastor's efforts and keep the lights on, keep the cameras running, and maybe sponsor a missionary or two that nobody really gets to know. Nope. Actually, when you read about the early church, it seems that God's dream is that every Christian would be unleashed in his or her calling, pursuing life on mission, and utilizing every gift and skill and experience and relational contact to build up the church and the kingdom of God. So the number one benefit of pushing back against the consumer model of church and striving toward a volunteer leadership culture is that it begins to redirect us back to God's original dream for his church.

Help People to Find Their Purpose

There are so many thrilling aspects to pastoral ministry. There's a certain thrill to delivering God's Word to a gathering of people, or pulling off an effective community outreach event, or offering biblical counsel to someone going through a difficult time, and certainly seeing someone take an initial step toward faith in Christ. But there are few things more thrilling to me than seeing someone find their God-ordained purpose in life. That happens over and over again in our approach to church. To sit across from someone as we together identify the ministry opportunity that God has for them at Grace and to see their eyes light up, and their heart beat fast, and their palms getting sweaty, and their shoulders straighten at the thought of being used by God in a significant way in his church. There's simply nothing like it. Church leaders, if you've never experienced that moment, it's time.

Make Your Church "Antifragile"

As I write this book, the world is in the throes of the first wave of COVID-19. We are on lockdown. Churches have closed their doors and moved operations online. The churches that make it through won't just need to be resilient, but they'll need to be what Nassim Taleb calls "antifragile" in his book by the same title.[20]

He argues that if fragile items break when exposed to stress, something that's the opposite of fragile wouldn't simply not break (thus staying the same) when put under pressure; rather, it should actually get stronger. Taleb suggests that it's no longer enough to bounce back from adversity and volatility or to simply be resilient. You have to bounce back stronger and better. This is what it means to become antifragile.

I'm convinced that high-capacity volunteer empowerment helps the church to become antifragile. Stronger through adversity. The church has already proven to be one of the most resilient institutions in all of history, but beyond just being resilient, I believe churches can become stronger because of one of the principles that Taleb discusses in his book.

He points out that antifragile things have built-in redundancies. Antifragile organizations sometimes tolerate being inefficient in order to have "layered redundancies." As Taleb notes: "Redundancy is ambiguous because it seems like a waste if nothing unusual happens. Except that something unusual happens—usually."[21]

Having redundancies doesn't just allow someone to survive a disaster but become stronger. A strong volunteer leadership culture builds necessary redundancies into the church. It provides multiple trained people who can step in and fill a role. It provides more engaged minds and hearts to speak into solutions. It provides more trustworthy, Holy Spirit empowered decision makers at the table to decide where to go next. I'm quite certain that we're going to come out the other side of the pandemic stronger because our high-capacity volunteers have helped to make us antifragile.

And not just during a global pandemic, these layers of redundant leadership will help us to continue to thrive in the midst of other sources of volatility. One of my main concerns for the modern church is its dependence upon the lead pastor. In smaller churches, because lead pastors tend to do everything. In larger churches, because lead pastors tend to achieve a celebrity status that becomes hard to replace should anything happen. In both cases, an army of high-capacity volunteers provides the scaffolding upon which to build the church's next chapter should anything happen to that key leader. At Grace, I'm convinced that if I croaked tomorrow, we wouldn't skip a beat, and we'd even grow stronger.

Accomplish More Ministry

The fourth benefit is very simple. But I don't want to overlook it or hurry past it. It's worth saying in plain language. Empowering more volunteer leaders will allow churches to accomplish more ministry. I'm certainly no math expert, but I'm pretty sure that all things being equal, two people can do more ministry than one person. And that five can do more than two and that ten can do more than five, and twenty more than ten.

In the Parable of the Soils, Jesus talks about spreading seeds somewhat indiscriminately onto four different kinds of soil. Only one of the soils is good and receives the seed and provides the proper environment for the seed to grow. But the other three kinds of soil all have issues that don't allow the seed to grow. So only one in four seeds grows. I'm not sure if you've ever thought about this through a ministry efficiency lens, but that's only a 25 percent success rate. It is a 25 percent return on the initial investment of seed. In some ways, it's comforting that Jesus seems to suggest that at least 75 percent of what we do in ministry won't work. It will be rejected, it will fall on deaf ears, people will get off to a good start and then fall away. But there is another very basic mathematical takeaway from this parable. It is simply this: if you want to see more results, you have to sow more seeds! If you sow eight seeds, two of them might take root. But if you sow twenty seeds, you may have five successes. If you sow a hundred seeds, you could see twenty-five plants growing. And one surefire way to sow more seeds is to enlist more sowers! More empowered leaders will allow your church to accomplish more ministry—it is simple math.

Develop a Deep Bench

A sports team is said to have a "deep bench" when it has a number of high-caliber players who are able to come into the game should one of the starters get injured or just need a rest. In 2018, Nick Foles led the Philadelphia Eagles to a series of playoff wins and eventually Super Bowl victory after the starting quarterback, Carson Wenz, got injured toward the end of the regular season. In fact, the team started wearing underdog masks because they were continually predicted to lose each game with Foles under center. But the Eagles kept winning. Why? Because they had a deep bench. High-caliber players who were developed and waiting in the wings.

One major benefit of nurturing a volunteer leadership culture is that it gives your church a deep bench. You have the chance to develop people in real ministry situations, so that when a ministry vacancy occurs, you will have a number of well-trained leaders to choose from. These leaders will be vetted, they are already familiar with the church's DNA, and you will have already observed them in challenging ministry environments. Some may turn down any offers to take a new position and will prefer to remain in their current role, but others will sense a calling from God and step up. In the last ten years, Grace has rarely looked outside to fill paying positions. Hiring from our deep bench has provided us with many talented, loyal, and long-term employees.

Fuel Engagement

Engagement is the new buzzword in church leadership circles. Similarly, customer engagement is one of the driving goals of every company in the world. Amazon, Starbucks, Chipotle, and every other successful company is obsessed with innovating new customer engagement strategies. In the church world, engagement is linked to things like attendance regularity, financial commitment, and key ministry involvement. Volunteer leadership is one of the best ways to get people deeply engaged in the life of the church. When a person has a seat at the table, and when they share ownership in the mission, the ripple effect from that deep engagement will be profound.

Get More Young Leaders at the Table

Recently David Kinnaman in conjunction with the Barna Research Group published a study called *The State of Pastors*. For years, there has been concern in the Catholic Church about the aging priesthood, but this report showed that there are early warning signs in the Protestant church as well. In 2017, the average age of a Protestant senior pastor was fifty-five, while just fifteen years earlier, in 1992, it was forty-four.[22]

Kinnaman explained some potential reasons on episode 125 of the Carey Nieuwhof Leadership Podcast. One reason is that older pastors, especially because of the 2008 financial recession, simply can't afford to retire as early as they used to. But another explanation is that ministry-minded Millennials are going into the marketplace and not ministry because full-time ministry is not as attractive as it was twenty-five years ago.[23]

These trends make engaging young leaders in ministry even more important. Volunteer leadership helps to bridge the gap for young people. Pastors know intuitively the importance of "keeping the church young." One of the places to start is to give Millennials and Gen Z a seat at the table. Invite them to step in to high-capacity roles, and then give them the two things many young people desire the most: freedom to work and spiritual mentoring. I would also add that it's important to resist the urge to pigeonhole young leaders in the areas of social media and video production. Ask them to speak into the preaching ministry, the leadership culture, and the future of the church.

Avoid Copycat Mode

A few years ago, I was on my way to South America with some other church leaders. On one of our flights, I was seated next to the director of content for a large Christian leadership conference. He was a young guy. His job was to read every book and article out there, listen to every podcast, and then secure the best potential speakers for this year's conference.

He and I started talking about the church. And I asked him, "What does a guy like you look for in a church to attend? You spend every day of your week reading and listening to the best communicators in the world—how could a local church pastor live up to that pressure each week?"

His answer was profound. He said, "People in my generation have access to the greatest content the world has to offer at the push of a button. We can listen to great preaching; we can listen to the best worship music in any preferred style at any moment during the week." Then he said, "I live in Atlanta, which has a collection of some of the most influential churches with the best bands and preachers in the whole country. But I don't go to any of them. I go to a little church in the city with one part-time pastor. The preaching isn't very good, and the music is very average compared to all that's out there. But there are three or four neighborhood ministries that are led by volunteers in my church that are making a huge impact in the city blocks right around the church. And none of those other churches can do that."

Many churches are just copying other churches. We go to conferences, we hear what the church in California or Atlanta or Chicago is doing, and we try to make it happen in our context. But the church is not a franchised content producer; it has always been an embodied localized mission. When volunteers are empowered to lead in the church, every church has a personalized fingerprint. The ministry is unique because each volunteer leader is unique. The ministry is local because each volunteer leader is local.

Pastors, if you want to break out of copycat mode and create something original, turn to your high-capacity volunteers. They probably won't know what LifeChurch is up to, or what Elevation or Hillsong did last weekend, but they will have a finger on the pulse of what God might want to do in your context. Every church is born an original; most die as copies. Let's reclaim the beautiful uniqueness of God's call on his church.

Part II

How to Develop a Volunteer Leadership Culture

CHAPTER 8

On Creating Culture

Volunteer leadership culture: A culture in which high-capacity volunteers (and not just paid staff) are entrusted with the responsibility of leading leaders.

Culture Is Critical

My family excitedly walked up to the new chain restaurant in town. It had gotten rave reviews from a few of my friends. I had heard that the food was great and the facility was new; what could go wrong? We opened the door on a Friday night, and we were the only ones there . . . *huge* red flag!

We approached the counter in order to build our own meal and found four employees engrossed in a conversation about their plans for later. Not one of them acknowledged our presence. Just when I broke the silence by saying, "We're here to order dinner," a fifth employee emerged from the back with clumps of meat in see-through plastic bags in a gelatinous sauce and proceeded to cut the bags open right in front of us and load them into the serving trays. There were many positive qualities about this restaurant—the building was beautiful, the furniture was new, the menu was nice, the processes were in place, the signage was clear—but the staff culture was really off. And culture is critical to a positive experience.

Creating a healthy culture in a church or changing an existing one doesn't happen by accident. It takes grit and intentionality. There are a number of intangibles that make up the culture of every church. They are the things that collectively cause a person to walk in and say, "This place just feels good, I love being here, it is so comfortable and welcoming." Or they may say, "This feels weird, something's off, it's making me uncomfortable." Which is what my family was saying as we witnessed the plastic bag meat ceremony.

When people think these thoughts and experience these feelings, what they're really evaluating is the organizational culture. Cultural factors include things like the environment, the spaces, the colors, proper signage, cleanliness, overall excellence, good processes, and the friendliness of all the people they encounter. These are all important, but culture is more than just the sum total of these things. And as a leader, you have a major say in what the culture is. If your church is going to pursue a volunteer leadership empowerment model, it all starts with culture.

Promote and Permit

You, as a leader, affect your culture by what you *promote* and what you *permit*. It comes down to what you reward and what you tolerate. Over time, what seem like inconsequential decisions or "we'll let it slide this time" moments can turn into a collection of intangibles that eventually become your culture. So, if you're trying to create excellence in your music ministry, while at the same time allowing Sister Bonnie's eleven-year-old niece to play her clarinet during the offering every week because you don't want to tick off Bonnie . . . well, by *permitting* her to play for those five ear-bleeding moments, you are undermining the culture of excellence you are trying to create. When there are behaviors that you don't like, but you tolerate, you are inadvertently creating culture. You can have great vision, mission, and values and still have a dysfunctional culture because of all the stuff that you permit.

On the other hand, if your main goal is to create a culture of intergenerational family worship, then your decision to spotlight your eleven-year-old instrumentalist will *promote* that culture. Every decision will contribute to the culture you are trying to create, either positively or negatively.

Volunteer Leadership Culture

So how does one create a volunteer leadership culture? Well, it begins with what you promote and what you permit. Some churches have settled into a spectator culture: everyone comes and watches the pastor do all the ministry. Some have embraced a foreign missions culture: the church hangs its hat on sending such-and-such percent of their annual budget oversees to missionaries. I've heard some foreign missionary culture advocates declare that they'd pay their missionaries before they'd pay the pastor or their mortgage payment. Some are committed to a worship excellence culture: the church is known for its incredible music and sound and lights, to the point where every musician and techie is paid to come in on Sundays, whether she is a Christian or not. These are examples of church cultures that have been created over time and are protected with fervor.

A couple of years into our commitment to volunteer leadership at Grace, I had a friend from out of town visit one of our Grace locations. I had a lightbulb moment toward the end of his morning when I realized that during his whole church experience, from the moment he walked in to when he left, he hadn't encountered one paid staff person. All volunteers. The guest experience team that greeted him, the children's workers that taught his kids, the entire worship band on stage, the preacher that morning, the Next Steps leaders, the cafe workers—all were volunteers. Not only that, but the staff overseers of each of those ministries (except worship) were volunteers as well. The entire site was being led and staffed by volunteers.

It made me think about some of the basic ways we *promoted* the values of a volunteer leadership culture in order for it to thrive. Some of these examples will be explored in the coming chapters, but let this be an overview:

- Preached regularly on spiritual gifts, personal calling, and servanthood.
- Provided ongoing opportunities for people to discover their ministry.

- Hosted ministry fairs where people could meet other ministry leaders.

- Highlighted easy-to-use digital opportunities for people to see and respond to needs.

- Offered regular stories of high-capacity volunteer leaders and the impact they're making.

- Changed our staff schedule to allow people who worked outside to participate.

It also made me think about the things we didn't *permit*. Things that could take root that might stand in the way of a thriving volunteer leadership culture. Things like:

- NO use of language like, "He's JUST a volunteer."
- NO different set of ethical or performance standards from staff to volunteer.
- NO micromanagement but instead empowerment.

Once the culture was established, there were some important steps we took that would allow volunteer leaders to thrive. Please understand many of these steps and principles were only gleaned and discovered in hindsight and upon reflection after the fact. This process for us was not a part of some strategic implementation plan. It was a lot of trial and error. A lot of one step forward and two steps back. Many of these lessons we're still learning and adjusting. Some are still in their infancy. But looking back now, it's evident that God has used each season and decision to engage more volunteer leaders for use in his kingdom.

CHAPTER 9

Step 1: Laying the Foundation

Establish Levels of Volunteering

There are some foundational decisions and practices that will begin to prepare your organization to implement a volunteer leadership culture. One of them is to decide on a trajectory of volunteerism that will allow people to ascend to a position of volunteer staff leadership. When we first started out, we skipped this stage of organization. But we've since found this kind of a framework very helpful in identifying and motivating volunteer leaders. The names and categories may change, but here is a sample of some levels of volunteering.

ENTRY—Temporary Team Member

It's very important to have a variety of temporary entry-level volunteer opportunities that anyone could step into. It allows people to feel and experience your volunteer culture, and it allows you to open the doors to untapped volunteers. These can be one-time roles that require very little commitment. Things like handing out programs at the big Christmas Eve service or manning the grill at the annual church picnic are good entry-level roles.

TEAM—Team Member

A team role is for those who wish to volunteer as a member of an existing team. They have made a commitment to be a part of your church and are willing to sign off on the requirements for joining an established team. It's important to have some intake process for these roles and an expected tenure of service, like once per month for a year. A team member might join something like the nursery team, the worship team, or the facility maintenance team.

LEAD—Team Leader

A lead role is reserved for those who are highly committed to your church and ready to accept the responsibility of influencing other people's lives. They will commit to ongoing leadership development opportunities and will be held accountable for doing their job well. These roles should be screened with an application, including references, and will probably involve other levels of legal screening. They will often have weekly responsibilities. Example roles: small group leader, children's ministry coordinator, leader of the guest experience teams (ushers and greeters), etc.

STAFF—Leader of Leaders

A staff role is for those high-capacity leaders with the time and skill to lead other leaders. They are entrusted with the spiritual and leadership development of those leaders under their care. They may oversee other volunteer leaders and may even oversee paid staff leaders as well. Because of their scope of influence, they will be considered part of the staff and will probably have daily ministry responsibilities. Staff leaders oversee things like the worship ministry at one of our locations, the youth ministry at one of our locations, or the small group coaching ministry.

Launch the Air Campaign

I remember being in my college dorm room watching the first "shock-and-awe" air campaign of the Iraq War on TV. The dark sky was lit up by missiles and bombs as they found their targets. In recent international conflicts, the US has adopted the strategy of "softening up the enemy" by waging relentless air strikes before the long and arduous process of taking new ground. The same principle applies when establishing a volunteer leadership culture in your church (without any violence or bloodshed, I hope!). Taking new ground will be easier with an upfront commitment to ongoing teaching and training on the subject of volunteer leadership and related topics.

If your church is going to adopt a new culture, at some level you as a leader have to speak it into existence with your own verbal air campaign. I'm not a big name-it-and-claim-it kind of guy, but I do recognize the power of speaking something into existence. When our daughter Ayden was young, we used to call her our "no drama girl." She was too young at the time to know how her personality would turn out, but we sure spoke as if it was true. She was going to be no-nonsense and no-drama! And sure enough—she's now a teenager with very little drama! Before our church was outward focused, I remember standing up every Sunday morning and welcoming all the first-time guests from the stage, giving them detailed instructions about what to do next. Here's the problem: there wasn't a single first-time guest in the room for months. But, soon enough our people started to invite guests—we spoke it into existence!

In the early days, we were committed to at least two four-week sermon series per year on the subject of spiritual gifts and servant leadership within the church. Preaching certainly isn't the end-all, but it is where a new culture begins. Your church needs to know that every person has a spiritual gift given by God, that each one has a role and a calling, and that the leaders have created space for high-capacity volunteers to assume significant ministry roles.

Listed below are some great passages and themes to use for sermons and trainings on volunteer leadership. You can also go to dereksanford.com for some sample message outlines.

- 1 Corinthians 12–14, "Every Believer Is a Minister." Ministry isn't reserved for those who get a paycheck from the church. Every person who believes in Jesus has a gift and a role.
- 1 Corinthians 3:21–4:2, "The Biggest Risk God Ever Took." God entrusted his followers to the roles of servants of Christ and stewards of the mysteries of God.
- Esther 4:11–17 - "For Such a Time as This." Finding and living your life's mission.
- Mark 5:18–20 - "Your Story Matters." You were saved to serve.
- 1 Peter 4:10 - "Get in the Game." Church isn't a spectator sport. Use whatever gifts you've been given to serve others.
- Matthew 25:14–30 - "When You're Entrusted with Much." God expects you to put to use the talents you've been entrusted with.
- 1 Timothy 4:14–15 - "All In." Don't neglect the gifts you've been given, instead immerse yourself in using and developing them.
- 2 Corinthians 9:6 - "Big Give." The law of the harvest is that when you sow generously with the ways God has gifted you there will be a great harvest.
- Romans 12:3–8 - "From Members to Partners." Christians aren't just called to be church members but ministry partners.
- Nehemiah 1:1–4 - "In You and Through You." Before God can use you mightily, He must break your heart about your true calling.

After you've softened up your church with the "air campaign" of preaching and training, a solid "ground campaign" is also important in terms of tactical systems and plans to mobilize an army of volunteers.

Begin the Ground Campaign: Assess the Landscape

After some initial teaching and training opportunities to the whole church, there are three critical assessments that must take place in order to prepare for a volunteer leadership culture as you look across the landscape of your church. You must assess ministries, systems, and leaders. Let me frame each assessment in the form of a crucial question.

Question 1: Which WELL-LED MINISTRIES would best facilitate our church's growth?

As you look across the landscape of your church, what ministries are missing or under-performing? What are the ministries that aren't thriving right now, but if they were thriving, they would give you some juice? What ministry, if it was well led, would have the best shot at moving the dial for your whole church? You need to identify your best ministry growth engines.

Some ministries are more important than others when it comes to a church's ability to make an impact. If you are trying to attract young families, a thriving kids ministry is key. If you want to focus on discipleship, then a small groups or mentoring program is critical. Part of the role of church leaders is to properly assess which ministries are most key to propel your church forward at this time. A good question to ask is "If we were starting the church over from scratch, which ministries would we begin with?" And then make a list in order of importance.

At Grace, when we first assessed our ministries, we recognized a number of ministries as potential growth engines, including small groups, ServErie (our community outreach ministry), and the worship ministry in one of our venues. Take small groups for example. We recognized that small-group discipleship was an area that was most strategic to our growth. We were attracting people but not retaining them, and we were entertaining people but not growing them. So, we needed a clear and focused ministry to disciple our people. Our assessment also pointed out that one of the reasons small groups were struggling was that there were other similar ministries competing for peoples' time and energy, like Sunday school and men's and women's groups. We would need to eliminate them in order to focus our efforts. In your situation, the best growth opportunities might be in youth ministry, college ministry, social justice ministry, men's ministry, or marriage ministry. Gather up some strategic leaders and ask, "Which well-led ministries would best facilitate our church's growth?"

Question 2: Which PROPERLY-FUNCTIONING SYSTEMS would help people take clear steps?
One of the most common reasons churches get stuck is that they have system problems. You can have great preaching, great worship, and engaging staff, but if certain systems aren't clarified and functioning properly, the church will remain stagnant. Does your church have a clearly defined, well-led system for first-time guests, new believers, first-time donors, people who want to be baptized, people looking for a group, people looking for care or counseling, people who want to volunteer, people interested in membership, and those who are ready to step into leadership?

Our assessment at Grace indicated a major gap in guest follow-up. We needed to put a flowchart in place. We had parts of a follow-up system, such as connection cards and material in the lobby. We even had a standard follow-up email from a pastor. However, these parts didn't effectively lead guests to take the next natural step. So we created a flowchart, identified missing or out-of-date steps, and improved the system. Now, guests have clear steps, and staff have a clear workflow to ensure no guest who wants to connect with us slips through the cracks. Our guest experience ministry leaders keep the system working smoothly and update it as needed. It's important for you to ask what systems, if they were properly functioning, would move your church's mission forward by helping people to take clear next steps toward growth.

Question 3: Which HIGH-CAPACITY VOLUNTEERS are not yet involved or fully utilized?
The final assessment has to do with people. It's just a good old-fashioned brainstorm session. If you lead a smaller church, you may be able to do this exercise alone. If you lead a larger church, you may need the help of others who are familiar with people in your congregation.

Consider those who are part of your church but are leveraging most of their leadership amperage outside your church. Maybe they run their own company or are a leader in their industry. Maybe they are an incredible parent raising great kids, a leader in their home. Maybe an effective teacher at a local school or a social worker that has mastered balancing multiple projects. Or a blue-collar worker who has demonstrated mastery within her industry. I'll spend some time in the next section talking about the anatomy of a high-capacity volunteer, but for now, simply ask, "Who could be leading in ministry, but they're not?"

Or maybe it's someone who is currently serving but is underutilized. They are handing out bulletins, but their capacity is much higher than that. Or they are setting up the coffee, or coordinating the communion team, but they have the potential for much more.

When our leadership team first did this exercise, we came up with thirteen names. Thirteen people we knew who had high-capacity volunteer potential but were either not involved or underutilized. These people included a partner of a local firm, an insurance agent, a recently retired executive, a homeschool educational coordinator, the general manager of a local restaurant, a stay-at-home mom, and a college professor. This brainstorm exercise of identifying untapped volunteer leaders is one our staff has repeated regularly since we did it the first time.

So assess the landscape of your church by looking at these three areas: ministries that are potential growth engines, systems that can be leveraged for advancement, and leaders in your congregation who are untapped. Before I talk about what to do with the results of these three assessments, let me pause to elaborate on what qualities make up a high-capacity volunteer. At Grace, we've been doing this long enough to know what generally works and what doesn't work when it comes to effective volunteer leaders.

The Anatomy of a High-Capacity Volunteer

When it comes to high-capacity volunteers, what should you be looking for? There are many important qualities that make up a high-capacity volunteer leader. But as our leaders looked across the landscape of volunteers serving most effectively, here are the five qualities we have found to be most important.

THE ANATOMY OF A HIGH-CAPACITY VOLUNTEER

Available Time

I would like to put something really spiritual at the top of this list, but time is really the most important quality! Most of our volunteer leaders put in between five and twenty-five volunteer hours per week for the church. Some categories of people who seem to have more available time are business owners, retired people, teachers and coaches, stay-at-home parents, and those who have a job that allows them to control their own schedule.

Red Flag: If they are already overcommitted and unwilling to drop something in order to assume the volunteer role.

Already Busy

Don't let the idea of "available time" fool you into thinking your best prospects are sitting around with their feet kicked up binge-watching Netflix series waiting for someone to ask. Most high-capacity leaders are high-capacity for a reason. They get stuff done! A lot of stuff. The temptation is to give up on them before you even ask because you assume that they'll be too busy to say yes to your proposal. Your best volunteer leaders are probably already busy with important projects personally or professionally, but if they are the right leader, a clear role and a compelling ask might just capture their attention.

Red Flag: If they have endless free time and are looking for something to fill it.

Passionate about the Mission

The best volunteer leaders grab ahold of the mission and vision of the church, and it ignites their imagination. If there aren't many people like that in your church, it may be that you haven't cast a clear vision or haven't regularly called people to the mission. The right volunteer leader won't try to shoehorn their own agenda or carry in baggage from the last church they served in. They will own the mission of your church at a deep level.

Red flag: If they are passionate about their own agenda or only recreating what they did at their last church.

Servant-Oriented

Jim Collins, in his excellent book *Good to Great,* describes a "level-five leader." Many people think that the most successful business leaders and CEOs are cutthroat and power-hungry. But Collins found that the leaders of good to great companies display a powerful mixture of personal humility and indomitable will. Jim Collins figured out what Jesus already knew and demonstrated: that great leaders will practice servanthood.[24]

Red Flag: If they seem always eager to have more power and authority.

Unoffendable

There are other words I could use to describe this quality. "Flexible" comes to mind, along with "loyal, patient, and thick-skinned." By the nature of their position, high-capacity volunteers are in a difficult spot. It would be easy to be offended by you or another church staff person, especially if they are coming from the business world and aren't familiar with ministry. They could also be offended by the people they are leading. We all know that ministry comes along with a huge target on your chest. Thin-skinned volunteer leaders will easily resort to "I'm not getting paid, I don't need to put up with this." The ones that will last are unoffendable.

Red Flag: They are easily frustrated and hard on people.

Match Your Growth Engines with Your Best Leaders

So, you've done your assessments. You have brainstormed ministry growth engines, system growth engines, and potential high-capacity volunteers. The next step is not rocket science . . . you simply match your growth engines with potential leaders.

At Grace, we made a two-column chart. On the left side, we listed the ministries and systems that needed leadership. And on the right side we listed the names of our leaders and we began to pray for God's guidance for the right people in the right roles.

Whatever you do, don't skip prayer. Just look to the example of Jesus to determine how important it is to pray before you choose your leaders. We saw earlier in Luke 6:12–13 that Jesus spent all night praying before he selected his new recruits. If that's true of Jesus, who is omniscient and omnipotent, I wonder how much you and I should devote ourselves to prayer, since we are more like _non_niscient and _im_potent. Ultimately, God knows what he is doing. It's his job to bring the right people to the right role. You need to tap into his heart and his mind regarding your future leaders.

So, after prayer and brainstorming, our first round of volunteer staff members began to take shape. Now all they had to do was agree to this crazy idea!

Create Clear Job Descriptions

Before you begin to recruit your new leaders, there is one very important resource you need to have ready: job descriptions.

Do you know what frustrates my wife? When I don't see what she sees. When we were first married and were cleaning the house together on a Saturday morning, I would occasionally ask her, "What do you want me to do next?" This was a perfectly reasonable question in my mind. Her response, however, went something like this with frustration in her voice, "Don't you see all the things that need to be done?" As a matter of fact, I didn't. I didn't notice to clean the front of the dishwasher with stainless steel spray, or that there were some crumbs under the cereal box in the pantry, or there was an envelope flap on the office counter that needs to be licked. She would say, "You mean to tell me you don't see those things?" The trouble is, I didn't see any of those things. It became clear that even though we were supposedly "one flesh," we weren't skilled at mind reading.

The same is true for high-capacity volunteers. Some will be willing to jump on board, but they can't read your mind. You need to write something simple and compelling to which they can say yes or no.

SAMPLE JOB DESCRIPTION

JOB DESCRIPTION
Position Title
GRACE CHURCH

ROLE IN ONE SENTENCE: (When someone asks what you do, this is the one sentence that captures it)

OWNERSHIP OF: (In simple terms and short sentences what are the areas of ministry that this position needs to own. This helps to provide clarity to the role – both for what it owns and what it does not.)

-
-
-

UNIQUE CONTRIBUTIONS: (What are the unique ministry tasks that the person filling this position brings to the team, regardless of their formal role? This section is more for paid and central staff for the purposes of leadership development. Remove this section for volunteer positions on teams, etc.)

-
-
-

RESPONSIBILITY STRUCTURE:
    I REPORT TO:

    REPORTS TO ME:

    REQUIRED MEETINGS (Lead / Attend)

    TIME EXPECTATIONS:

We use a very basic job description for both paid and volunteer leaders. It includes four key parts:

- **The role in one sentence.** Try to narrow down the goal of the job in a simple statement.
- **Basic responsibilities.** Two to three bullet points summarizing general job responsibilities.

- **Reporting.** Who they report to and who reports to them, and how often.

- **Time commitment.** Give a range of expected hours per week that the job will require.

If having a job description scares them off because it makes the job "too formal" or it freaks them out to have too much responsibility, they are probably the wrong person for the job!

Once your job description is ready, it's time to make the big Ask.

Doris

Meet Doris

Doris's "real" job: Currently retired. Was operations director for a major insurance company for over twenty years.

Doris's volunteer role: Next Steps Ministry

How did you begin in this role at the church? "We often read about baby boomers finding their 'second career'— sometimes by lending expertise in our field and other times being able to experience something very different than our past. After being an operations director, I knew I needed to do something more meaningful, something that had true and lasting consequences. I earned a good salary, which made me want to be *sure* this was a God call, and not just a passing thought. It seemed like a lot to give up (as if my needs were met by me instead of God)! It was also daunting to think about changing from a fast-paced environment with measurable metrics, business conferences, and upward mobility potential. Yet when I talked to my executive pastor about serving in a high-capacity volunteer role, I walked away intrigued and excited! As one of the first volunteer staff, I had the chance to help mold what the roles would look like, which was energizing."

How were you made to feel like a part of the staff? "I wasn't sure how I'd fit in since I was twenty-plus years older than most of the staff. But the generational mix was all part of God's plan. Their energy prompted me, and I hope I passed along some wisdom that comes with age and experience to the next generation. I didn't feel as though I was volunteering; instead I felt I was an integral part of the team, because I was treated like a legitimate staff member. (I was given a workspace, office equipment, systems access, and meeting participation.) I was fortunate to also experience a career path since the team practices ongoing leadership development and serving in the area of our gifts. I started leading Next Steps (discipleship) ministries, which later morphed into a one-on-one coaching ministry. How thankful I've been to see God change what I thought was my life's work into a ministry that challenges me, strengthens my faith, and affirms what God had in mind for me!"

CHAPTER 10

Step 2: The Art of the Ask

Make It a Big Deal

The first step in inviting a potential high-capacity volunteer to serve in a critical role is to help them understand that it is a big deal. This isn't just another invitation to do a mundane church task one per month. This is a big deal.

Imagine that you were bringing in a candidate from another part of the country and trying to convince them to accept a paid assignment at your church. You would roll out the red carpet, you would plan ahead for your conversations, take them out to the best restaurant in town, make their spouse feel special and included. You need to approach these asks with that same mentality. It's not a text message, or an email, or a "let's grab ten minutes in my office after the service on Sunday." You need to make it special. The atmosphere of the ask needs to match the responsibility of the role.

Invite them to your home for a meal and a conversation, take them to a fancy restaurant, involve their spouse, maybe involve another colleague from your team. Many of our initial recruitment conversations were paired with a free ticket to the Global Leadership Summit simply as a token of thanks for hearing us out with this crazy new idea. Make sure you are ready to present them with a simple job description, but it needs to feel like a really big deal. Because it is.

Avoid Recruitment Traps

There are some common traps that you should avoid when making an important ask.

The Saying-No-for-Them Trap

It's very tempting to say someone's no for them. However, you have to resist filling your mind with reasons this person could turn you down. You can convince yourself that they're too busy, or they're at the wrong stage of life, or they have too many other irons in the fire, or they don't really like you. But if you go into the ask with this mindset, it will be very difficult to make a compelling case for the role.

The Soft-Sell Trap

Some leaders try to soft sell the role that they are asking a volunteer to step into. They say things like "This won't take much time at all," or "you should be able to squeeze this into your normal schedule," or "you could do this in your sleep!" If you are a leader yourself, you know that these kinds of phrases are *not* motivating. Leaders want to hear that there is a big problem to solve, a dilemma to figure out, and that it will take their best time, their best energy, and some sacrifice to pull it off. And in the end, there will be a kingdom-sized payoff! Don't soft sell the ask, because real leaders like a challenge. Plus, if you soft sell the role and they agree to it, at the first sign of difficulty, they will quit. Because, hey, this was supposed to be easy—and it turned out to be hard.

The Guilt Trap

Church leaders have become quite proficient at guilt motivation, and it almost always backfires. "I need you to lead the children's ministry because if you don't, all these little kids are going to wind up pregnant or on drugs." Or "You should lead the visitation ministry because how dare you ignore your elders who have done so much for you. They went to Vietnam for you, so stop being so entitled and volunteer for them." Guilt might be strong enough to convince someone to start leading, but it won't sustain their leading.

The Victim Trap

Don't go into a big ask and tell your potential volunteer leader how worn out you are. How being a pastor is so overwhelming that no one could understand what you're going through and you just need a little help to keep your head above water. Most volunteer leaders won't be motivated to join in on what appears to be a sinking ship. High-capacity leaders are drawn to other high-capacity leaders, so they need to see how you are attacking big problems and how they are part of the solution. Don't play the victim card.

The Cattle-Call Trap

Finally, these big asks need to happen one-on-one. It's quicker and easier to stand up on a Sunday morning and announce the need to the whole congregation, hoping that someone might step up—a diamond in the rough. But the problem with a cattle-call approach is that, while it gets the word out to everyone at once, it also communicates that any old person with a pulse could do this role. A one-on-one meeting gives you a chance to look someone in the eye and tell them, "I think you are perfect for this role. No one could do this like you could. Do you think God might be calling you to this?"

It's critical to avoid these recruitment traps, they never end well.

Connect Their Role to a Clear Vision

A man came upon a construction site where three people were working. He asked the first, "What are you doing?" and the first worker replied: "I am laying bricks." He asked the second, "What are you doing?" and the second worker replied: "I am building a wall." As he approached the third, he heard him humming a tune as he troweled on the mortar and then set the brick in place. The man asked, "What are you doing?" The third worker stood up straight, looked up at the sky, and smiled, "I am building a cathedral!"

This is an old story that has made the rounds from sermon illustrations to corporate training events. But it points out the importance of a big-picture perspective in the work that we do. When it comes to inviting high-capacity volunteers into a new role, it's important to give them the vision of the "cathedral" they will be building. You must paint the picture of how their role will impact the larger vision or mission of the church. Leaders don't always respond to need, but they are more likely to respond to vision.

Make sure you are able to articulate how the behind-the-scenes accounting and bookkeeping role will allow your church to continue to change people's lives. Remind them how the children's ministry role will impact the trajectory of families for generations to come. You have to remind them that you're not just asking them to lay bricks; you're inviting them to build a cathedral.

When we relaunched our small group ministry and began to recruit our volunteer leadership team, I presented to them again the mission of our church, which is to make and to be fully devoted followers of Jesus. Then I added that, unfortunately, our church had succumbed to a spectator model. People would come for services, enjoy the music and teaching, and then pass each other like ships in the night on the way to their cars. They weren't growing as disciples, and they weren't discipling others. But, I asserted, as more and more people connect with one another in the comfort of a living room around some food, and share life together, and Scripture, and prayer, and accountability, suddenly the great commission of Jesus will begin to come to life. Groups will become the greenhouse for spiritual growth in our church.

In pursuit of this dream, our goal was to move from 30 percent of our church to 80 percent of our church in life groups in one year. To accomplish this, we needed small group leaders committed to providing safe gathering spaces and facilitating sometimes tough conversations—leaders eager to invest in their growth and the growth of other Christians. That team of leaders chased after that dream: they could see the cathedral. They recruited the additional needed high-capacity leaders by connecting their role to a bigger vision that we were all chasing together. By the end of the year, we had 83 percent of our congregation engaged in a small group.

Be Completely Honest

It's tempting to sugarcoat things when you ask someone to take on a critical role, but you must be brutally honest. If the person is right for the role, they will appreciate it, and it will set the proper tone going forward.

When you present the simple job description, be honest. When you estimate the number of hours it will take, be honest. When you describe the current culture that they'll be stepping into, be honest. When it comes to your own strengths and weaknesses, be honest. We have found that anytime there is fuzziness in communication or expectations up front, it leads to dysfunction later. So just be honest.

Don't Be Afraid to Pull Back

My wife Kim and I were flying from Ft. Lauderdale into Philly. Our plane had made its final approach to the runway, the landing gear was down, and we were in that moment when the wheels were just about to touch the ground when the pilot violently pulled the plane back up. In fact, we were pointing so straight up in the air, I had that weightless feeling in my stomach like we were about to plummet backward down to the earth. Thankfully, we didn't. When we started circling again and people stopped screaming and collecting themselves, the pilot came on the speaker and said something like, "You may have noticed that we were going to land and didn't." Ummm . . . yeah . . . we noticed! "But," he said, "just as we were about to touch down, it became clear that the plane in front of us hadn't cleared the runway, and if we had continued with the landing, there would have been a collision, so we had to abandon the landing at the last minute."

After gathering myself, I realized I had learned an important leadership lesson that day. It's better to pull out of a situation at the last minute, even if it's awkward or uncomfortable, than to have it end in disaster.

This is also true when you're making an ask of a potential high-capacity volunteer leader. If during the course of the conversation, the fit just doesn't seem right, it's OK to pull back. You can simply say, "I thought this was going to be the right fit, but based on where you're at, or based on what you just said, or based on your time capacity, I just don't think this is going to be the right thing for you to step into right now." It may be slightly uncomfortable, but if it saves a crash later, it will have been well worth it. The best time to deal with a bad fit is before someone is on the team. It may also be a great opportunity for you to redirect them to another area of ministry that would be perfect for them.

God Will Go Ahead of You

One of my favorite New Testament stories about the art of the ask is that of Ananias and Saul. Ananias is only mentioned one time in the whole Bible, but he was given an extremely difficult assignment by God. Saul, the murderer of Christians (soon to be the Apostle Paul), had just seen a bright light on his way to Damascus. He was blinded and sent into hiding for a few days. Then God comes to Ananias with a tough assignment. God said, "I want you to go to public enemy number one, the guy who has been running around and killing every Christian he can get his hands on, and I want you to help him take his next step of faith." Here is the exact wording from Acts 9:11–12:

> And the Lord said to him, "Rise and go to the street called Straight, and at the house of Judas look for a man of Tarsus named Saul, for behold, he is praying, and he has seen in a vision a man named Ananias come in and lay his hands on him so that he might regain his sight."

And Ananias is like, "I don't like this assignment, God. I've seen the grainy YouTube videos of this guy lining up people on the beach and pulling off their hoods and killing them. He's a terrorist. You've got the wrong guy, God. How about this instead—how about I just pray for him. I'll give lots of thoughts and prayers for Saul. Or how about I serve you some other way. . . . I'll lead a small group, or maybe this—I'll dust off my tuba from high school band and offer my services to the worship team. But please send someone else to invite Charles Manson into pastoral ministry."

God says, "No. Here's the address. Here's what the house looks like and the person's name who owns it. I want you to walk through his front door, give him his sight back, give him some food, baptize him, and pave the way for him to change the world in my name." And did you notice the detail in verse twelve? God had already told Saul that Ananias was coming! He had already paved the way. We should take great comfort in the fact that God has gone ahead of our ask. He has been doing the work of preparation despite our hesitation.

Listen to God's response to Ananias's protests in Acts 9:15:

> But the Lord said to him, "Go [that doesn't leave much wiggle room], for he is a chosen instrument of mine to carry my name before the Gentiles and kings and the children of Israel. . . .

God says, "I've got big plans for Saul. First, I'm going to change his name to Paul, and then he's going to impact *all the gentiles and kings and the children of Israel.* That's pretty much the whole world. Paul's story will become one of the great arguments in history for the power of the cross and the truth of Christianity. The greatest enemy of Jesus became the greatest force for Jesus when he encountered the power of Jesus. And Ananias was the one who would get to extend the invitation.

So, Ananias obeys God. He goes to Saul, he makes the ask, and the rest is history.

I'm amazed how many times I have invited someone to lead in ministry, and they respond with "God has been preparing me to say yes to this."

What if You Don't Ask?

Using the example of Ananias and Saul, I want to end this section on the Art of the Ask by attempting to stiffen the spine of those who still may be hesitant to invite someone into a significant leadership role without pay. Let's simply consider: what if you don't ask?

I mentioned that, earlier in the story, God had already prepared Saul by revealing to him that a man named Ananias was coming. God had prepared Saul for Ananias's arrival.

That first step across the threshold and into the house must have been the scariest for Ananias. What was going through his mind? He probably kept saying "it's not about me, it's not about me, it's not about me." He had no idea what he was going to find. Was it all a trap? Would Saul lash out at him, reject him, kill him? Or was this the real deal?

After working up the courage to enter, Ananias sees a guy sitting in the middle of the room with his head bowed. He puts his hand on Saul's shoulder, startles him out of his meditative prayer, and says to this terrorist who had been killing anyone associated with Jesus, "Jesus sent me to you"—*It's not about me, it's not about me, it's not about me*— "and Saul, God wants you to receive your sight back, oh and receive the Holy Spirit, oh and feel free to share with anyone who will listen about this Jesus." Saul's sight comes back. He's baptized and he grabs some food. And proceeds to turn the world upside down with the gospel. Even though he doesn't receive much credit, the ordinary obedience of Ananias would change the course of history.

Can you imagine if Ananias hadn't asked? Can you imagine how the growth of the early church would have stalled if Ananias had been too scared, or too preoccupied, or too proud, or too negative, to go and pave the way for Saul to change the world? God could have used anyone for this history-altering assignment, so maybe nothing would have changed too much if Ananias backed out—but he chose to use Ananias. Can you imagine how disappointed Ananias would have been to miss out on this moment? But God had prepared Saul for this visit, and Ananias obeyed.

God has placed people all around you who will help you to chase down God's vision. God has prepared them for you by softening their spirit and working on their character. He's directed you to ask them. All that's left is for you to ask. Instead of worrying that they might turn you down, instead of fretting about the potential awkwardness of the conver-sation, consider what your whole church might miss if you chicken out. What partnership might you miss out on if you fail to engage them? What calling might they miss out on because of your hesitancy? Even scarier than wondering how the conversation will go if you *do* ask them to lead, is considering what will happen if you *don't*?

CHAPTER 11

Step 3: Setting up for Success

Transition to a Volunteer-Friendly Schedule

So, your brand-new high-capacity volunteer leader said yes! You made a convincing ask, you gave them a clear role and a simple job description—now, how do you set them up for success?

One of the first major changes we had to make within our leadership structure was the rescheduling of our regular staff meetings. It had been on Tuesday afternoons at 1:00 p.m., but if we were going to have an influx of volunteer leaders, we would have to reconsider the time. Most of our new leaders had other jobs, many of them 9:00–5:00, so although a Tuesday afternoon staff meeting was very convenient for our paid staff, it wouldn't work for our volunteer staff.

So, we moved our monthly staff meeting to Tuesdays from 5:30 p.m. to 7:30 p.m., and we threw in a dinner for good measure. At first, the prospect of an additional evening commitment put off our paid staff a little, but soon they saw the positives far outweighed the negatives. We were inviting in so much more manpower and adding so much more leadership voltage to our team. Ultimately, our staff understood that this move would allow us to accomplish much more ministry.

These days, our full-staff meetings are quarterly instead of monthly. And all key meetings are scheduled with volunteers in mind. Some happen over lunch hours; some happen through video chat. One of the early sacrifices we made—and that you'll need to make to set up your culture for success—is to make sure the schedule is conducive for key volunteer leaders to be in key conversations.

Delegate Authority, Not Tasks

Craig Groeschel put words to this important concept in an episode of his leadership podcast, "It's About Time, Part 2." He insightfully says, "Delegating tasks creates followers, but delegating authority creates leaders."[25]

So, if you find yourself telling a volunteer leader, "I need you to go set this event up exactly this way," or "I want you to run the numbers that way," or "Lead the team for me this way," ultimately you will train people to do what they're told. And this approach might work for your boots-on-the-ground volunteers: the folks who want to help the church and just need regular clear direction. But when it comes to high-capacity volunteer leaders, they need to be involved earlier in the process and given a different level of ownership. You don't want them to be followers only; you need them to be leaders. This means it's important to delegate authority and not just tasks. Here are a few ways we have practiced delegating authority.

Involve Them in Defining the Problem

Instead of handing them a to-do list that you've created, invite them to define the problem with you and brainstorm potential solutions. This will allow you to observe them in action, and them to observe how you think about ministry. So, agree together on the problem—this is the first challenge. Then you let them pray about it and ask them, "How do you think we should address this problem?"

Years ago, I asked Jim to lead the effort of mobilizing our church in regular acts of community service. I was convinced that our people were a little lazy in their faith. Too comfortable enjoying the "good life" to lend a hand on a Saturday morning. Instead of tasking Jim with an in-your-face recruitment campaign, I remember asking him, "Why don't the people of our church show up to serve our city?" His answer shocked me: "I have found that most people who don't live in the city are too intimidated to drive in the city, to try to find parking, afraid to drive the wrong way down a one-way street, and then show up late and flustered to a community agency they'd never been to and try to get their heart into doing some community service." That's a completely different problem than spiritual laziness!

Because Jim was involved in defining the problem, he then felt empowered to solve it. He was given authority to help create ServErie Saturdays. In the end, he proposed renting school busses to solve the transportation problem. He also wanted to place a guide on each bus to introduce participants to the mission and vision of the agency they would be serving that day. It was a brilliant solution to a problem that I wasn't even aware of. Some adjustments were needed along the way, but Jim was emboldened to solve them because he had been involved from the ground floor. This process will take some time up front as you develop trust and synergy, but the payoff in the end will be more than worth it.

Transfer Authority Publicly

It is critical that when it's time for a new leader to lead, you, or whomever is seen as the existing authority for that ministry, make a public transfer of authority. There is some historical and biblical precedent for this kind of public transfer of authority. Back in the Middle Ages when it was time for a squire to step up and become a knight, there was a public ceremony, often called an accolade or a dubbing ceremony, where someone in authority would lay a blade on the shoulder of the prospect in order to confer knighthood.[26] In the Bible, the leaders of the church in Antioch laid their hands on Paul and Barnabas before sending them off on their first missionary journey in the authority of the church.

I'm not suggesting a dubbing ceremony for your new volunteer youth leaders or even anything as formal as an anointing or hand-laying. But there is something important about a formalized handing-over-of-authority from one to another. This doesn't need to happen in front of the whole church, but there is certainly a team or a group of people who would benefit from hearing about this new leader and their new role from some authority figure.

So, call together the team and say something like, "We brought you together for an exciting announcement—Kristen has agreed to a role on our staff that will involve leading this team. Here are the reasons we think Kristen is the perfect fit for this role. And even though Kristen may not be getting paid, she is a full-fledged member of our staff, so you can look to her as your staff leader. She has walked through a process to take on this role, and I couldn't be more excited about the impact she's going to make as the leader of this ministry. I would ask you that whatever respect and authority you have given to me, please give to her. She has the full authority to make decisions as it relates to this ministry. If you have any encouragement, or suggestions, or problems, you should take them directly to her and not to me. I have full confidence that God is going to do great things through you all as you work together." And then you give Kristen a chance to address the team and cast some vision for what she hopes the team will accomplish together. Especially early on in the culture-building process, this public transfer is critical to that new volunteer leader's success.

Practice Situational Authority

Nikki was the new volunteer leader of our biggest leadership development event of the year. She was getting ready to lead the first team meeting. Nikki had confessed to my assistant prior to the team meeting that she was very nervous because I, the lead pastor, was going to be in attendance. I was invited to attend this initial meeting simply to connect the dots from this event to the larger vision that our church was chasing. When I heard of her nervousness, I reminded her that we practice "situational authority," meaning that even though I may be the "higher ranking" staff person in the room, in this case she is the one in authority. I would simply be in the meeting to share my piece of the agenda. If any questions would arise, they were hers to answer. Inevitably during the meeting, one participant gave some pushback that required a decision. All heads in the room turned to me. That moment gave me a chance in front of the whole team to affirm

Nikki's authority as leader of this event and that her opinion weighs more than mine right now in this room. Scenarios like this have been a great opportunity to delegate authority and not just tasks.

Say "You Decide" often

Volunteer leaders are going to be tempted to turn to you like a security blanket with every question and every decision that needs to be made. The best two words that you have in your arsenal are these: "You decide." In a truly empowered culture, you should be saying, "you decide" far more often than you are offering your own opinion.

Determine "the Fence"

If you are a parent of small kids, you understand the blessing of a fence around the backyard. Without a fence, you are consumed with where your kids are at all times. Did they run out into the street? Did they escape to the neighbor's? Did they mindlessly wander down the sidewalk never to be seen again? It's hard to make dinner, fold laundry, or read a book if you're constantly fixated on the kids' whereabouts. To a parent, the fence represents safety—it represents security and the ability to get other things done worry free while the kids have a blast in the backyard.

In order to truly empower volunteer leaders, it's important to create a sort of fence where they can play freely. Within the fence they can lead, they can innovate, they can freely make decisions. But it will also provide the proper boundaries to protect your church from unnecessary confusion and complexity.

Our executive pastor, Aaron, innovated this concept of the fence for our context. It has gone through a number of iterations over the years, and there is no perfect model, but consider these four sides of the fence:

Side 1—Mission and Vision

Is it consistent with what we are doing and where we are going as a church?

Side 2—Values

Is it consistent with who we are and what's important to us?

Side 3—Simple Structure

Is it doable without adding complexity, confusion, or financial strain to our existing structure?

Side 4—Team

Is it endorsed by and does it fit the scope of your job within the team around you?

Within those four sides of the fence, anything goes. Innovation is encouraged, and independent decisions can be made. But when an idea violates the boundaries of the fence, there are conversations and corrective actions.

The truth is, sometimes fences, no matter how spacious the yard, feel restrictive to those playing within their borders. Some leaders will want to spend their time and energy challenging the fence. They will want to pursue ideas or agendas that fall outside the scope of your mission or values. Or spend their time duplicating efforts with what others on the team are already working on. Certainly, it can be helpful to revisit the parameters of the fence from time to time. But the sooner you can communicate and gain agreement on the fence, the sooner a leader can begin to play and thrive within its boundaries.

Create an Onboarding Process

Having a plan for onboarding your new volunteer staff leaders is another way to set them up for success. Think about the impact of an effective on-ramp to your staff. It has the potential to ensure that they feel welcomed, set them up to "win," increase their engagement and satisfaction, improve their performance, increase their retention, and reduce the time it takes them to "hit the ground running."

A great onboarding process accomplishes all of these things while also minimizing frustration and the initial awkwardness that can come with a new role and new environment. It's easy to understand the importance of this in a paid job, but in a volunteer leadership role, I would argue it's even more important. Here are some questions to wrestle with as you consider how to best onboard volunteer leaders:

- How will we make a fantastic first impression?
- Who is the perfect person to walk them through the onboarding process?
- Who should they talk to in the first week?
- What do they need to know about our culture/values?
- What do they need to know about our expectations?
- Will we provide them a workspace onsite?
- What tools will they need to succeed? (computer, iPad, keys to the building, business cards, access code to the copier)
- What is the communication expectation? (Will they have a company email address, a phone extension? Will they be expected to use their personal cell / personal email?)
- What do we hope they will accomplish in their first month?
- Do they have information for their key contacts and key meetings?
- Have we provided all proper paperwork? (clearances, moral standards documents, staff policy manual, job description, etc.)

Embrace Intentional Inefficiency

Equipping volunteer leaders usually won't feel like the straightest path to your destination. It takes a lot of effort and time, especially early in the process. During a volunteer leader's onboarding process and in the weeks and months to come there will be many days that feel inefficient. You have to help them understand the values and the culture, you have to instill some history and experience, you have to walk by their side and coach them through things you could do in your sleep. There will come plenty of moments where you will say, "This would be so much easier if I just did it myself." And that is true . . . in the short term. But the day will come when you will be able to hand that ministry off completely, and if all goes well, you won't have to think much about it going forward because a well-equipped leader is handling it. So, for a while it will feel inefficient, but it's an intentional inefficiency as you press on toward the payoff.

Blur the Lines between Paid and Unpaid

One of the key shifts that helped to set us up for maximum success with our volunteer leadership culture was when we began to blur the lines between paid and unpaid staff. I already talked about the importance of creating a friendly volunteer rhythm when it comes to meetings. Changing our staff meeting to the evening was a very important step in this direction. But there are several other decisions that can help to make this shift.

Watch Your Language

I don't mean stop cursing about your leaders (feel free to keep doing that!). One of the key language violations that we started to police in the early days was the phrase "*just* a volunteer." As in, "We can't expect Tyler to do good work / show up on time / be prepared / because Tyler is '*just* a volunteer.'" This kind of unintentional verbal slip will begin to negatively affect the empowering culture you are trying to build.

Publicly List Paid and Unpaid Staff Together

Wherever the list of your leadership team appears on your website or church bulletin, simply list paid and unpaid staff together with no designations. For some reason, the temptation is to point out that certain people aren't paid. So we'll stick a big *V* next to their name for "volunteer." If you are trying to establish a volunteer leadership culture, take the *V* off the tag line and just call them "staff."

Be Generous with Staff Amenities

Give your volunteer leaders an official church email address, give them a workstation, a box of business cards, a phone extension, and a formal name badge. All of these things demonstrate to them that you are serious about their contribution in this role. It also helps them to take the role seriously and invest significant time and energy back. If you are thinking, "We don't have the money to get business cards or add another official email address," just remember how much you are saving by not having to pay their part-time salary! Another step we've taken is to provide professional childcare at certain times throughout the week so that volunteer staff with young children can work onsite without having to find their own childcare. Again, the cost for this amenity pales in comparison to what you would actually pay these leaders for their time.

Rethink Internal Communications

One of the lessons we learned along the way was that we needed to include our volunteer staff in enough internal communication that they felt in the loop, but not so much that they felt overwhelmed by an inbox filled with unnecessary staff chatter. Moving most of our ministry communication to task-based apps has helped this. Utilizing a project-based resource like Microsoft Teams or Basecamp is an important step to take. This assures that most communication is focused on the projects they're working on and minimizes the need for constant email updates. Email is then reserved for broad communication and telling stories of God's greatness.

Expect Them to Abide by Staff Policies

This might be the hardest on the list, and we have achieved it with varying levels of success. But a key step in blurring the lines between paid and unpaid is holding your volunteer leaders to the same policies and procedures as your paid leaders, including things like performance reviews and vacation requests. As strange as it feels to require someone who is not receiving a paycheck to turn in a vacation request, it is completely necessary if your volunteer leadership culture is going to succeed. If someone is legitimately fulfilling a key role on your staff, you need to know when they'll be gone. And if their vacation falls at a bad time, you need to be able to negotiate that with them, too. Also, include your volunteer leaders in the regular rhythm of performance reviews. Just like other staff members, they deserve to know how they're doing and what needs to improve. The more you normalize these behaviors, the less awkward they will feel to everyone.

Provide On-Time Training

I pursued my undergraduate and graduate degrees on two totally different paths. My BA was a traditional on-campus four-year degree. But my master's took—well, let's just say a much longer time. I was on the thirteen-year plan. But while plodding through my master's degree Bible and theology classes, I was also in the middle of doing ministry. I found it to be a much more effective way to learn, because in addition to acquiring information, I was able to immediately test out my newfound knowledge with hands-on application in real ministry situations. It was a great approach to training.

In his helpful book *Sticky Church*, Larry Osborne refers to "need-to-know and need-to-grow" learning. In talking about spiritual growth and maturity, he says that most spiritual growth doesn't come as a result of a linear program or a set curriculum. It comes as a result of life putting us in a need-to-know or need-to grow situation. Osborne describes need-to-know as "a predicament where we need to know God's viewpoint" and need-to-grow as "a tough trial or a stretching experience." Traditional education tells us, in Osborne's words, "Take good notes now, because someday you'll really need this stuff!" [27] But true learning and training seems to happen best when you are in situations where your only two options are to learn and grow or to fail.

The same principles are true when it comes to leadership training and development. There is a place for formal training, but for volunteer leaders, some of the best training comes on the job and on time. Below I list out some of the ongoing training opportunities we have provided for our volunteer leaders. They range in variety from informal to formal.

Regular Check-ins

Each leader has regular check-ins with their supervisor. A good check-in on our team includes some version of the following categories and questions:

Personal:
- How are you personally and spiritually?
- How is your family?

Progress Report:
- What can we celebrate?
- What progress are you making on goals/ assignments?
- What challenges are you facing in achieving your goals?

Next Steps:
- How can you build on progress and/or address challenges?
- What are the new goals and initiatives you are chasing?
- Is there anything we're avoiding saying that needs to be said?

Resourcing:
- How can I help? What do you need from me?
- How are your key volunteers?
- Who on your team could be better utilized or equipped?

Key Takeaways:
- What are your key wins between now and our next check-in?
- End every check-in with prayer.

Relevant Training in Meetings

We want to take advantage of the times when our volunteers are already gathered. So, we like to incorporate a short, relevant training component into full staff meetings and other team meetings. This takes some energy and foresight. We will often talk together and get feedback one to two weeks ahead of meetings to decide what the most needed training topic is at the time. We ask, "What does our team need to hear? Where do we need to grow?" In this way our training is on time.

Access to Do-It-Yourself Resources

We subscribe to both Right Now Media and Leadership Book Summaries. Both have excellent, easily navigable leadership resources. It is easy to refer any leader to relevant training at one of these sites. There are also any number of podcasts with helpful ministry training that are free and accessible to all. Some of my favorites are the Craig Groeschel Leadership Podcast, the Carey Nieuwhof Leadership Podcast, the Andy Stanley Leadership Podcast, and unSeminary Podcast with Rich Birch. All of these resources can be excellent for a leader and his or her supervisor to listen to or read on their own before discussing what they learned.

Read a Book: Ask Two Questions

This is a simple but very helpful approach from Dan Reiland. You can do this one-on-one or with a small team. Dan suggests assigning a book (or book summary) to read together. Then meet together to answer two questions: 1) what did you learn, and 2) how are you applying it?[28]

Leadership One Days

As our volunteer staff has grown, we have added a quarterly Saturday morning training event called Leadership One Day. There are four fifty-minute training sessions between 8:00 a.m. and noon on a Saturday morning. These leadership lessons are facilitated by leaders from our church as well as local experts from our community. All training topics are handcrafted to be immediately relevant to our leaders' current circumstances. And our leaders can choose which session(s) they will attend from just one to all four during the course of the morning.

Church Leadership Class

Finally, we use a curriculum that I wrote as my master's thesis (yes, the thirteen-year plan produced at least one resource of value!). It is a graduate-level class on church leadership, complete with out-of-class assignments, in-class lectures, and cohort discussion groups. We offer this class at least once per year for those who are recommended by our leadership team (a mix of both paid and unpaid leaders) for next-level training and development.

Kerrie

Meet Kerrie

Kerrie's "real" job: Community School Director. Kerrie works for the United Way of Erie County providing engagement, volunteer, and educational opportunities for families within a small school district and the surrounding community.

Kerrie's volunteer role: Head Trainer for Small Group Ministry

How did you begin in this role at the church? "I was invited to sit with two of our Grace staff members. The invitation was very relaxed, yet extremely honest with expectations. It was such a humbling moment for me when I was asked to help get this new direction started for such a big ministry. Never would I have thought that I could help lead this. However, having two staff members that I respected and cared for present to me why they wanted me to be a part of it was very energizing to say 'yes' to the ask."

What was intimidating about what you were asked to lead? "The most intimidating part was wondering how I was going to find time. And how I would find the right approach to make the ask (to other potential leaders), how I would learn to be understanding and patient when the answer was 'not now,' and to not become overwhelmed or discouraged. The larger team hadn't been built yet, so it was literally starting with one person which was super energizing and scary all at the same time."

How is being a non-paid staff member hard? "When meetings are held during the day, I can't participate in them. As my ministry has changed and evolved over the last five years, there have been a few times when a decision was made that I had questions about, but by the time I could get to the emails and get caught up, we had already moved onto the next item. I have had to find the balance between digging my heels in and going with the flow. It is really important for me to understand the 'why.' Once I do, then I can pass that on to leaders and coaches so that they can be on board too."

What would you say to others who might be considering a high-capacity volunteer role at their church? "Don't be afraid to say 'yes' to the opportunity. Praying over the ask is *so* important. It is such a humbling moment when people you love and respect tell you what they see in you and that you could add value to a ministry. To use your gifts and time to serve others can fill your bucket in ways you may not realize you need to be filled up. Be open and honest about what excites you and overwhelms you. Open communication is critical. Know your limits and share them, honestly. The more open your eyes are walking into the ministry role, the more fulfilling and God honoring it will be."

CHAPTER 12

Step 4: Staying Power

The Retention Challenge

One of the most difficult challenges of a volunteer leadership culture is the long-term retention of volunteers in leadership roles. In our case, the turnover of our volunteer leaders has been much higher than that of our paid staff. The longevity of our volunteer staff leaders is approximately eighteen months on average.

On the other hand, we have some high-capacity volunteer staff who have remained in their roles much longer than that. I recently gathered about ten of them in a room and asked, "What factors have contributed to you staying in your role for this long?" It was a fascinating conversation. Their responses will be sprinkled through the sections in this chapter, but one response rose to the top in a unanimous chorus.

Each of them said passionately, through the lens of their individual experience, something along these lines: "I'm doing this to serve God."

Each could point back to a seminal moment when they realized God had not only entrusted them with a spiritual gift but also given them leadership influence that could be leveraged for his kingdom. In some cases, this was a personal revelation; in others, it was a sit-down with a pastor or ministry leader. But in each case, there was a lightbulb moment of personal calling. One of the volunteer leaders even had the audacity to say to me, "I have to remind myself regularly that I'm not doing this for you, Derek. I'm doing this because God has called me to this role." I joked about being offended, but I was so encouraged.

This meeting was an important reminder for me that no matter how impressive our systems are, and no matter how polished our strategies are, the key ingredient in this whole volunteer leadership endeavor is the Holy Spirit of God. Nothing can replace the power of his calling and the sustaining impact of his presence. Which means that of all the practical ideas offered in this book, the greatest work of a pastor or church leader is to continue to point our volunteer leaders back to God and his calling on their life. We need to encourage their faith at every turn. And one of the greatest gifts we can give them is the gift of intercessory prayer.

Pray for Them

There are many ways to care for people in your ministry; the most powerful has to be intercessory prayer. Begin by just writing down a list of your key leaders in a journal, or put their names on the whiteboard in your office, or on the home screen of your phone, or a 3 × 5 card on your dashboard, and commit yourself to pray for them. When volunteer leaders step up into ministry, they instantly put a bullseye on their own chest and on their family. We need to stand beside them in prayer.

And when you pray for them, don't get sucked into just praying the two common American prayers. I call them the big two—safety and comfort. If aliens came from outer space and listened to most of our prayers, they would think that the goal of the Christian life is for everyone to be safe and comfortable. The problem is, when I read the Bible, I don't see either of those two things anywhere close to the top of the list of desired outcomes.

Just look at two different passages to get a glimpse of the kinds of things that Paul prayed for those under his leadership. These prayers can act as a kind of model for us to follow. He demonstrates both the frequency of his prayers (in bold) and the content of his prayers. You can judge for yourself, but I don't see a hint of "safety" or "comfort": anywhere.

Colossians 1:9–12:

> For this reason, since the day we heard about you, **we have not stopped praying for you** and asking God to fill you with the knowledge of his will through all spiritual wisdom and understanding. And we pray this in order that you may live a life worthy of the Lord and may please him in every way: bearing fruit in every good work, growing in the knowledge of God, being strengthened with all power according to his glorious might so that you may have great endurance and patience, and joyfully giving thanks to the Father, who has qualified you to share in the inheritance of the saints in the kingdom of light.

Ephesians 1:15–21

> For this reason, ever since I heard about your faith in the Lord Jesus and your love for all the saints, **I have not stopped giving thanks for you, remembering you in my prayers**. I keep asking that the God of our Lord Jesus Christ, the glorious Father, may give you the Spirit of wisdom and revelation, so that you may know him better. I pray also that the eyes of your heart may be enlightened in order that you may know the hope to which he has called you, the riches of his glorious inheritance in the saints, and his incomparably great power for us who believe. That power is like the working of his mighty strength, which he exerted in Christ when he raised him from the dead and seated him at his right hand in the heavenly realms, far above all rule and authority, power and dominion, and every title that can be given, not only in the present age but also in the one to come.

I would encourage you to use these passages, like I have many times, as models and starting points for your prayers for volunteer leaders. Because I believe that if God grants your leaders these things, the Holy Spirit will continue to sustain them for ministry longevity and effectiveness.

Let Them Lead

Another factor that will supply staying power for your volunteer leaders is simply giving them freedom to lead. If they feel micromanaged or controlled instead of empowered and supported, I can almost guarantee their term of service will be short. Empowerment has two common enemies that can show up in your own spirit when you release new volunteers to lead. The two enemies are insecurity and pressure. When either of these two appear in your life, your knee-jerk reaction will be heavy-handed control. But no one—and especially no true leader—likes to serve with a controlling fellow leader.[29]

If you resort to control, it will have a negative impact on your staff's leadership. First, they will become tentative and indecisive. They will lack the confidence to move ahead with initiatives. And I don't know about you, but I would much rather have to pull back the reins because someone is going too fast than have to light a fire under their butt because they're too slow and tentative.

You will never attract, build, and retain great leaders unless you release some controls and free them to lead.

Encourage Them Often

Leading and motivating volunteer leaders is one of the greatest leadership challenges in the world. I'm convinced of it. If you own a business, there are myriad ways that you can encourage and motivate your employees. Most have to do with financial incentives: year-end bonuses, raises, and stock options. In a paying job, the motivation factor can be pretty straightforward: if you perform well, you will get more money. If you perform poorly, you will get fired. It's as simple as that. But with volunteer leaders, it's important to develop a whole different toolbox for attracting, motivating, resourcing, and retaining them to achieve high performance. So, when you remove the financial motivator, how is it that you keep a small army of volunteer leaders fired up? Encourage them often. What follows are some encouragement ideas, and the key to all of them lies not in the expense but in the genuineness of the sentiment.[30]

Send a Handwritten Note of Thanks

Just ten years ago, this idea would have been so obvious it wouldn't have even been included on a list like this. But in the digital age of email and texting and social media, handwritten notes have become a rare treat.

As we packed up my middle son for college this year, I spent a lot of time in his room. When I looked at his corkboard wall of mementos, I couldn't help but notice something that looked out of place. There among his sports medals, the pictures of his closest friends, and trinkets from his favorite trips, hung a notecard with our church's logo. It was a handwritten note from a volunteer team leader thanking Chase for his selfless service. A handwritten note made it to my teenage son's wall of fame. Our church's elders have adopted a habit of signing and sending three personalized thank-you notes to a volunteer leader each month. I often see these notes posted on people's refrigerators or featured in glowing social media posts because the handwritten note, sent through snail mail, meant so much to them.

Brag about Them in Front of Them

If you have access to a pulpit and a microphone each week, use some of your airtime to brag about specific volunteer leaders. Otherwise, catch them doing something right and tell others about it while they're within earshot. In the hallways of our church, I try to introduce our volunteer leaders to guests or other team members by calling to mind something that leader has done that impacted lives. I'll often say, "This is Joe—he is one of the key reasons that our church is thriving and having such a huge impact in our community."

Invite Them to Enjoyable Experiences

Our staff Christmas party has become a can't-miss event for both our paid and unpaid staff. In addition to a great meal, there are competitions, awesome gifts and prizes, tons of laughter, and great stories and recollections from another year of ministry together. Our teams have had pool parties, worship parties, bowling trips, escape rooms, ice cream truck visits. Heck, one year we had a crawfish boil—which in Northwest Pennsylvania is quite a feat! The point is, one of the ways to encourage your leaders is by giving them experiences that are enjoyable and encouraging.

Thank the Employer or Coworkers at Their "Real Job"

Most secular companies and employers encourage their employees to volunteer in the community. A simple email to your volunteer leader's employer outlining the impact they are having at your organization can go a long way to increasing their stature and reputation at their workplace. One of our most committed volunteer leaders is a partner in a local firm. Each year during their busiest week, we send in a spread of bagels and pastries to his whole office of colleagues and employees to express our appreciation that they share their boss with our church so willingly.

Tell Stories of Life Change

One of the most rewarding acts of encouragement is simply to share stories of life change with your volunteer leaders. Remind them that they are part of God's great work in the world. These stories remind them that what they are doing is worth it. All the extra time and energy, all the sacrifices that they make in order to serve, are accomplishing something. Many of our pastors send out a weekly email to their volunteer leaders for the sole purpose of telling inspiring stories from the previous week. You'd be amazed at the motivational impact of this practice. It's like getting a non-financial bonus every single Monday!

Share a Gift of Love

A gift certificate for a night away without kids at the movies or the philharmonic, dinner out, a bed and breakfast getaway, five free coffees at Starbucks: these gifts of love communicate appreciation to key leaders. There are plenty of other options that don't cost money, like inviting the children from the kid's ministry to create a card for their teacher, or youth to provide free babysitting for their small group leaders. Write a funny poem or sappy song expressing your admiration for your team. These gifts of love won't soon be forgotten.

Do Something Nice for Their Family

Every time I've written a note to the spouse of one of my key leaders, it's been met with heartfelt thanks. Sometimes spouses and families don't realize what kind of impact their loved one is having through their volunteering. Provide a family picnic or day at the beach or a local theme park, tickets to the local fair, or a family movie night. Make sure whatever you do includes an explanation of the powerful value of volunteerism that their family member is demonstrating.

Post Pictures

Secure a photographer to take pictures of the leader and their team in action. Celebrate them publicly on social media. Or give that leader access to the church's social media story page so that they can do a day-in-the-life feature. This will allow you to celebrate the leader while allowing them to bring recognition and promotion to their ministry area.

Expect a Lot

This should be clear from all that's been written so far, but most true leaders appreciate and respond to high expectations. As our society has seemingly adopted a "setting the bar low" mentality, with an entire generation receiving participation trophies, there has been a quiet resurgence of research in the arena of setting high expectations for school students.[31]

It turns out that when teachers have high expectations for students, it actually builds the student's self-esteem, increases confidence, and improves overall academic performance. This isn't just true for grade school students—it's true for human beings of all stripes and especially true of leaders. Leaders love to step up to challenges; they appreciate high expectations.

One of the common refrains from my meeting with our long-term volunteer leaders was this very truth. They appreciated that we had entrusted them with big challenges and expected them to lead well and come through. We created a positive environment for them to serve and then assumed the best about their ability to achieve results.

There is supporting research for this idea. A Gallup Leadership Institute meta study found that the Pygmalion Effect (or Self-fulfilling Prophecy Effect) has a very strong impact on human performance among leaders.[32] Here's how it works. In one particular study, half of the leaders were told they would be working with exceptional teammates. They were told that their group was better, smarter, and more motivated than the rest. They were supposedly the high achievers. This was all nonsense. The other leaders were told nothing at all about their teams. In reality, the teams were randomly selected, and neither was better or worse in its makeup than the other. But the leaders approached their groups with the preconceived notions they were given by the study team. And in the end, the teams' actual performances were substantially different—the so-called "superstars" performed like superstars. The other group performed like an average group.

What was the difference? There was a high expectation placed on one group and no expectation placed on the other. And the high expectation proved to be a motivating factor that positively impacted the group's performance. Don't be afraid to expect a lot from your volunteer leaders as it will press them to be great.

Celebrate Every Victory

Some people are "celebration challenged." They have a tendency to focus on tasks without celebrating the successes. They are quick to try to correct what's not working rather than to revel in what God is up to. Or so I've heard!

. . . Fine, yes, it's true, I count myself among the celebration challenged.

I have to be reminded that it's not prideful or unspiritual to stop and celebrate spiritual victories and the people who contributed to them. God seems to reinforce this notion. In God's economy, celebrating spiritual progress actually combats pride because it turns our attention to God's faithfulness and turns our hearts from pride to gratitude.

Throughout the Old Testament, God instituted a rhythm of celebration through the annual religious calendar of his people the Israelites. There were seven specific feasts,[33] four in the spring and three in the fall. These feasts and festivals were an opportunity to stop, look back, and celebrate what God had done. Along with these scheduled moments of celebration were God's regular commands to remember and celebrate him.

In Deuteronomy 8, the Israelites are preparing to enter the promised land after generations of trials and tribulations. Moses puts the people on an extended pause. God challenges the people about the importance of remembering:

> And you shall eat and be full, and you shall bless the LORD your God for the good land he has given you. "Take care lest you forget the LORD *your God* . . . lest, when you have eaten and are full and have built good houses and live in them, and when your herds and flocks multiply and your silver and gold is multiplied and all that you have is multiplied, then your heart be lifted up, and you forget the LORD your God, who brought you out of the land of Egypt, out of the house of slavery, . . ." (v. 10–14)

Later, in Joshua 3–4, God performed an amazing miracle for his people. He caused the Jordan River to stop flowing so they could cross on dry ground into the promised land. God then instructed them to gather twelve stones from the Jordan to set up as a memorial. Joshua set them up as a sign, as a remembrance, of what God accomplished for his people on that day.

The alternative to properly celebrating and giving God credit for our victories is giving ourselves credit for all that has taken place. See, not only does stopping to celebrate what God is doing help to motivate our volunteer leaders to keep going, but it also helps us to combat pride and arrogance in subconsciously thinking that our ministry successes are due to our own cleverness and hard work.

We love having members of our church come into our volunteer celebration events to share stories of what God is doing in their lives. Not only does God get the glory, but our volunteers are filled up knowing that their investment of time is making a difference.

Reinforce the Big Picture

I popped into a regularly scheduled meeting of our small group coaches. These are the people who support and coach our small group leaders. The team of coaches was being led by one of our outstanding high-capacity volunteers. As I observed the meeting, I was so impressed with the skillful way in which Doris led the meeting. She provided biblical foundations, created an environment for collaboration and mutual support, and offered skills-based training for the task at hand. At one point, she turned to me and asked me if I wanted to share a word of encouragement with the team. I think it turned out to be a word of encouragement for her as well.

I reminded them of the reason that we created this team of coaches. We had discovered that the best shot we have at making disciples—the key component of our church's mission—is getting people into a group. But not just any old group. We found that the common factor among groups who were making great disciples was they all had a leader who was on fire for Jesus. So we created this team of coaches to keep our leaders fired up in their faith. Lightbulbs started turning on around the room in the eyes of those coaches. I wasn't telling them something that they didn't know already—they had just forgotten because vision leaks. I reinforced the big picture of why their job was so important.

I've found as a leader that one of my most important jobs with our volunteer leaders is to continue to reinforce the vision to them. I need to remind them as often as possible that there is a bigger story being written to which they are contributing. And if I can tell that story to them in front of their team, even better. One of the factors in retaining volunteer leaders is reminding them often that their role is connected to a bigger picture.

Provide Real-Time Coaching

I love preaching in African American churches. In one sense it's terrifying, but in another, it's exhilarating because I can always count on getting real-time feedback. People in the congregation actually talk back to you! If you're on a roll, you'll hear things like "Go ahead preacher," or "Preach on prophet," or "Oh here we go . . . stay right there," or my personal favorite, "You meddlin' now." You always know just where you stand. I asked one of my Black pastor friends if he ever gets negative feedback while preaching. He told me a story of an old lady in the front row one Sunday. The preacher had lost the crowd and was really bombing. The old lady in the front simply said matter-of-factly, "Oh Jesus, help him." You'll get feedback, and it's immediate, not like in a white church where you have to wait for a few days and then receive it in your inbox.

When it comes to job performance, people don't generally clamor for feedback, even though there are many opportunities to offer it. If you go to a restaurant, you may get a card at the end of your meal asking for feedback on your dining experience; or if you receive tech support online, you can answer a few questions at the end to rate how helpful your technician was; college students can evaluate their professors with an anonymous feedback system. Often, people don't take the time to give feedback unless they had an unusually bad experience. It's why when you pull a leader aside and say, "I'm going to give you some feedback," their first reaction is probably not eager anticipation. More like preparation for carnage.

The problem with instant feedback when it comes to job performance is that it often calls out a problem without offering a solution. That's why coaching is a much better alternative to feedback. Your volunteer leaders need real-time coaching. Marcus Buckingham describes a year as fifty-two sprints.[34] Each week is an opportunity to push forward life-changing initiatives. He says that feedback is like a grenade that you throw over a fence[35] (often once per year at performance review time). But what your leaders really want is for you to come back to their side of the fence and provide some coaching. His recommendation is to ask two questions each week:

1. What are your priorities this week, and
2. How can I help?[36]

This kind of real-time support empowers your leaders to lead, but it also positions you to be there for them in a coaching posture.

There is a more robust coaching approach (beyond Buckingham's two questions) that we've used over the years with high-capacity volunteer leaders. This method, 5R Coaching, comes from Robert Logan's book *Coaching 101*.[37] He encourages supervisors to base their coaching agenda around the 5 *Rs*: Relate. Reflect. Refocus. Resource. Review. Real-time coaching allows you to stay engaged with your volunteer leaders and helps them to keep serving for the long haul.

Assist with Evaluation

While coaching focuses on an individual leader and her specific leadership challenges, she will also need help and support in inviting evaluation. Evaluation includes the larger teams she is leading and focuses more on the effectiveness of programs and other initiatives. Both of these processes help volunteer leaders to stay in the game by obtaining real-time feedback and a sense of personal growth and ministry improvement.

After every event or initiative, we try to gather people who were involved for an evaluation session. All feedback is on the table. The good, the bad, and the ugly. We try to major on honesty and minor on defensiveness because we know that the truth will make us better. Volunteer leaders are introduced to the importance and expectation of constant evaluation.

When other pastors and church leaders visit our staff and get a taste of our culture, they inevitably think that we're a little "extra" about evaluation. Our executive pastor, Aaron, practically bursts through my door after every staff meeting or training event, asking, "How did it go? What can I/we do better?" We try to evaluate after every weekend worship service. If we can do it a little better the next time, why wouldn't we? Lives and eternities are at stake, after all! Every church picnic, baptism service, and Christmas program is run through the wringer of evaluation.

But inviting evaluation is a challenge because it puts everyone in a vulnerable position. And it's not always fun to be vulnerable. Sometimes, inviting others' opinions about the success or failure of an endeavor is painful. Especially when it's something that the leader is personally connected to. So, leaders tend to avoid evaluation for at least three reasons:

1. It takes extra time that we feel we don't have.
2. We don't care what other people have to say.
3. We are too insecure to hear others' opinions.

Leaders will be especially eager to avoid the evaluation process if they already know the initiative didn't go well. It's easy to believe that you just don't need someone else's voice to tell you that it failed. You are well aware.

Yet the value of constant evaluation is incredible. It provides a win-win-win: The team wins, the ministry wins, and the leader wins.

The team wins: Team members are reminded that their opinion is valuable. They have a seat at the table, so they feel included. The event or ministry wins: It will be made more excellent and effective the next time because of the constructive feedback that's offered. And the leader wins. Each high-capacity volunteer will get better as a leader and will earn more trust from their team just by asking for input, even if they already know what the team will say.

So, one of the gifts that you can give your volunteer leaders is to assist them in inviting evaluation. This also helps you as their supervisor: You gain fuel for encouraging them, and you also won't have to initiate every difficult conversation with them. Some of the negative inputs will come from others on their team, and you can just come alongside and help them process the information and implement necessary changes.

There are two different kinds of evaluation that we practice. Ongoing ministry evaluation, which happens as often as needed throughout the year, and then annual ministry evaluation. Each one uses a different tool.

Ongoing Ministry Evaluation: Four Questions

This ministry evaluation matrix is based on four questions. We use these questions after programs, events, weekend services, team meetings, etc. to frame our feedback:

- What went right?
- What went wrong?
- What was missing?
- What was confusing?

Annual Ministry Evaluation: SWOT Analysis

A broader tool that we use annually or biannually to evaluate an entire department or ministry team is the SWOT analysis. This process helps to provide a big-picture look at our children's ministry, or worship ministry, or operations department. An evaluation like this usually involves getting the key leaders together for a two or three hour brainstorm session and working through their feedback. A SWOT analysis provides a great structure for team evaluation and communication, and then a helpful discussion tool for you and the volunteer leader. This analysis tool allows a team to gauge their strengths, weaknesses, opportunities, and threats:

Strengths (internal)

- What advantages do we have?
- What do we do better than anyone else?
- What unique resources can we draw upon that others can't?
- What are people in our ministry excited about?
- Why are people attracted to our ministry over other options?

Weaknesses (internal)

- Where do we keep coming up short?
- What could we improve?
- What do people in our ministry see as detrimental?
- What factors make us lose ground?

Opportunities (external)

- What good opportunities can we spot in the community? Local events?
- What relevant local/national trends are we aware of?
- What changes have we noticed in the world around us that our ministry might address?

Threats (external)

- What obstacles do we face?
- Are there any cultural trends or changes that are threatening our ministry's effectiveness?
- Do we have any negative financial trends or problems?

This tool is a great jumping-off point for conversation. Then after the initial brainstorm, when it comes to interpreting and applying the data, it's helpful to match up your strengths and opportunities. Ask, "What do we do really well, and where could we leverage our strengths in the world around us?" Also match your weaknesses and threats. Ask, "Where are we already vulnerable, and how could we mitigate external risks?" After doing this basic analysis work, you can create strategies and goals out of your conclusions to build on your strengths and minimize your weaknesses.

Can You Fire a Volunteer Leader?

Whenever I talk to other pastors or ministry leaders about volunteer leadership, this question comes up. And the answer is, "Yes . . . but it's tricky." It seems a bit counterintuitive that you would let someone go when they're working for free! But sometimes it's critical to do so.

The thing you have to keep in mind is that you are the keeper of a culture. We learned earlier that a culture is a combination of what you promote and what you permit. So if one of your volunteer leaders turns out to be a bad fit, or they turn out to be an underperformer, or they have a toxic personality, and you permit them to continue, you are sowing negative seeds into your culture. And culture is contagious. Soon others on the team will start exhibiting those same negative behaviors.

So, how do you end well with a volunteer leader? First, you need to define *why* things aren't working. This will give you confidence as you deal with the situation, and it will also give you a framework around which you can build a constructive conversation.

Carey Nieuwhof defines three potential problems that could require a removal:

- **A character issue**—lacks moral judgment, work ethic, or trustworthiness.
- **A competency issue**—lacks the skills needed for the job.
- **A chemistry issue**—lacks the right relational or organizational fit[38]

Once you've defined the problem, a direct conversation is the next step. The conversation should be face to face. It shouldn't be long, and you should spend some time first outlining the things you love and appreciate about the person and the work they've done in ministry. It is good to write these positive things down so you can give them to the leader or send them in a follow-up note. They probably won't remember any of those things by the end of the conversation.

After that, the volunteer leader deserves a frank conversation about why things didn't work. It will help them develop as a leader in the future. It's also important during this conversation for you to own the things that you did wrong in the process. A bad placement is never entirely the fault of the person that was placed.

If the problem is competency or chemistry, and there is another potential spot for this volunteer leader to serve, be prepared to recommend a different role on the spot. If the problem is a character issue, come prepared with an action plan that may help them work through the particular issue that they are struggling with.

If this meeting goes right, it will feel like the volunteer leader was more prepared for the conversation than you were. They will have sensed the bad fit along the way, or they will have become acutely aware that they don't possess the proper skills for the role. Often the leader will be more than willing to try another leadership role after a short break to catch their breath.

If it goes badly, which it does sometimes, it will usually involve the volunteer leader crying foul on other team members. They may accuse you or the church of "using" or "taking advantage" of people. Hidden bitterness may rise to the surface, and it may become clear that the person was resentful because they weren't being paid for their time, or that they were mistreated by their supervisor. A healthy culture can withstand a few of these incidents. Usually people on the team are familiar with those involved and can withstand the relational or emotional fallout that's created by the difficult conversation. And usually team members were aware long before you that things weren't working.

We have had very few of these situations so far at Grace. For the most part, our leaders have served with passion and effectiveness. When they have needed to take a break, they have, often to return in another crucial role in another season.

CHAPTER 13

Step 5: Equip, Unleash, Repeat

A Constant Process

Aaron coined the motto "equip, unleash, repeat," which has become a rallying cry for our team. He has lived out the reality that in order for a volunteer leadership culture to grow, take root, and thrive, there needs to be a constant flow of new leaders. Raising up people, equipping them for ministry, and then unleashing them into meaningful service. But it can't stop there. The process needs to repeat itself again and again until the culture takes root deep in the organization. Otherwise the culture will become stagnant and stuck. Allow me to use two water analogies to illustrate.

Tale of Two Seas

There are two big bodies of water in Israel: the Sea of Galilee and the Dead Sea. I've had the privilege of visiting both. The Sea of Galilee, famous for Jesus' storm-napping and Peter's water-walking, has a number of rivers flowing into it. At the same time, the Jordan River flows out of it to the south. The Sea of Galilee is a beautiful, healthy body of water with an abundance of sea life.

The Dead Sea also has rivers flowing into it. But nothing flows out. It's a dead-end. Consequently, the mineral content has become so high, it seems like it's transforming from a liquid to a solid. When you wade into the Dead Sea, it feels like slogging through Jell-O. You can even lay on top of the water and stay afloat because the water is so dense with sediment. It's a sensation that's hard to describe. And because of the salt concentration, nothing living can survive in its waters. There is no animal life, no plant life, no fish, no birds, no underwater seaweed. The sea is not called "dead" for nothing! The simple conclusion in comparing these two seas is that for life to flourish, there has to be both inflow and outflow. Where there is inflow and no outflow, there is only death.

The same can be said for many Christians in many churches. They seem lifeless because they have collected the inflow of content at church for their whole lives, hearing sermon after sermon. They learn truths and sing songs. They experience life and learn from their experiences, but they neglect to pass on their knowledge and experience to others through service. There is inflow, but no outflow. And the sad result is a sedentary kind of spiritual deadness. In order for a sea, or a Christian, to be healthy, there must be a healthy outflow of serving, mentoring, and investing in others. Achieving the proper outflow isn't just critical for an individual Christian life; it's also critical for a successful, life-sustaining ministry and organizational health.

A River or a Puddle

A river is an incredible thing. Water that is constantly dancing over rocks and boulders, flowing and moving to the next bend. Rivers attract and produce life. The Amazon basin has the highest concentration of rivers in the world. It holds more species of plant and animal life and produces more of the earth's oxygen than any other place in the world. These rivers create movement and vitality, constant replenishment. An abundance of rivers means an abundance of life.

A puddle is a different story. Puddles are created by some depression on the surface of the earth or a parking lot or sidewalk. The water that collects in a puddle is still and stagnant. It's shallow and warm. And aside from the occasional insect skimming across the surface or a bird cleaning its feathers, a puddle is relatively lifeless. There is no movement or flow, there's no abundance, no life.

Is your ministry more like a puddle or a river? Is it stagnant or thriving? Is there inactivity or vitality? The life-giving flow of an organization happens through its people. So, we've adopted the Equip, Unleash, Repeat approach because it creates forward movement in our culture. When a high-capacity volunteer steps into a new role, it's important for them to be *equipped* to do the job well and *unleashed* with authority to fulfill their role. We want their ministry to thrive and succeed. We want them to set direction, make decisions, and lead their teams with excellence. But there's one more thing that mustn't be forgotten (and it's easy to forget): We also want them to be thinking from their first day on the job, "How can I *repeat* this process with someone else who could one day take my place?" This mentality keeps the organizational river flowing. Not only will that volunteer leader eventually step out and create a new position for the next great leader, but as soon as she identifies that next leader and equips him and unleashes him, she will have also freed herself to step into another high-capacity role. And the river dances on toward the next bend.

The bottom line is that every leader in our church has two jobs. She needs to do the job that is outlined on her job description, and she needs to raise up and empower her replacement.

This ever-flowing river of leaders has another benefit. This process allows the church to stay current and relevant in our rapidly changing world. The flow brings new life. It nurtures new young leaders who have new ideas about how to reach our culture, how to disciple young Christians, how to approach music and creativity, how to harness social media. If we remain a stagnant puddle, we will not only cut ourselves off from high-impact people, but we will also cut off the flow of new life and new approaches to ministry. And our churches will soon find ourselves in the predicament that the US Military recently did when it entered a war on terror in which the enemy didn't play by the traditional rules of engagement. In the words of General McCrystal in his insightful book *Team of Teams*, we are in danger of developing "tremendous competencies for dealing with a world that no longer exists."[39] The world is rapidly changing all around us. The church must not settle for being relevant to a world that no longer exists. Instead, we must encourage a constant flow of new leaders. Equip, Unleash, Repeat.

Finding Your Replacement

It sounds a little deranged. In fact, you probably wouldn't be able to get away with it in a normal job. But we encourage all our leaders to work on finding their replacement from the start. One of their key jobs is to work themselves out of a job. If they don't, they may easily find themselves feeling overwhelmed, frustrated, and alone.

The Old Testament prophet Elijah had some unforgettable experiences.[40] He spent some time hiding out in seclusion at the brook of Cherith, where he was miraculously fed by ravens. When the brook dried up, God moved Elijah to the widow's house in Zarephath, where he performed miracles with the replenishing of flour and oil and the resurrection of the widow's son. He then saw the enemies of God defeated as fire fell from the heavens on the top of Mount Caramel. He prayed and rain came to the land and ended three and a half years of drought. That's a solid run—a pretty good ministry resume. But those miracles only led to new attacks by the evil queen Jezebel, and Elijah found himself in a position of depression and loneliness.

So, Elijah took up his complaint with God, trying to convince God that he was the only faithful leader left in the land. In response, God sent a strong wind, a powerful earthquake, and a blistering fire, but God was not found in any of the three elements. He was found in a gentle whisper in which Elijah heard the voice of God. This inaugurated a season of replenishment in which God responded to Elijah's discouragement. I find it fascinating that God didn't give him a new ministry assignment or magically heal his depression. Instead, God told Elijah to go find his replacement. He sent him to anoint Elisha as a prophet to take his place.

In order for God to continue to do his work in the world and in his church, we must be open to a constant replacement process. God still provides leaders with an Elisha if they will listen to his voice. Often an Elisha may not be a likely candidate, but through prayer, God will reveal his choice servant who will be perfect to repeat the process of empowerment so that forward motion will continue to flow through the church.

Practice the Apprentice Model

My wife is not tech savvy at all. To this day, even though she's been doing it for many years, I still have to help her with email attachments. She types text messages with her pointer finger only, or if she uses the voice feature, she adds every punctuation mark, much to our teenagers' delight. And sometimes she gets confused between text messages and phone voicemails. She famously left a voicemail on the work phone of one of her business associates with full punctuation. "Hi Joe, comma, this is Kim period. I was wondering if you could call me back within the hour, question mark." You get the picture.

I'll never forget the day I walked in on a conversation between Kim and her seventy-something-year-old mother. Kim was in full tech-support mode. You see, her mom's phone "wasn't working." In this case, "wasn't working" just meant her phone needed to be powered on. But I was so proud because when I walked in, Kim had already solved the powering-on situation and had then moved on to teaching her the ins and outs of how to open and view a picture when it's texted to her and a variety of other basic mobile phone lessons.

This scene reminded me of an important truth: it doesn't matter how little you know—to someone, you're an expert! If you've been doing a task for a week, you're an expert to the person who's only been doing it for an hour. To her mom, Kim was as good as the Geek Squad.

In fact, the best downhill ski instructors for novice skiers often aren't the professionals but the ones who just learned to ski last winter. The one-year veterans have a better shot at explaining skiing to the rookies in a way that they'll understand. Which is why the apprentice model is so important in ministry.

If a volunteer leader has been doing ministry for any amount of time, to someone, they're the expert. Volunteer leaders often push back when it comes to training their replacement by saying, "I don't even know what *I'm* doing yet." But in many cases, it's better that way. They are in the perfect position to bring someone else along. This is why it's important to practice the apprentice process. The apprentice model is very simple. It follows a five-step pattern:

I do. You watch.

Apprentice is in observation mode only and should write down questions. We debrief.

I do. You help.

Give the apprentice a specific job to do, but the leader is still doing the main job.

You do. I help.

The leader releases the main responsibilities to the apprentice while still doing a secondary job. We debrief.

You do. I watch.

Now the leader is only observing and taking notes for a debrief. The leader should resist the urge to step in and solve problems unless there is a disaster brewing. We debrief.

You do. Someone else watches.

This is where the process comes full circle. The former apprentice is now leading and begins developing a new apprentice.

This process takes time but is a powerful way to establish the flowing river of new leaders and new ideas.

The Story of ServErie

I'll never forget the scene. I showed up at one of our underfunded urban schools in downtown Erie. It was midsummer, so school was not in session. Thousands of volunteers were scurrying around the hallways and grounds as part of a massive cleanup and revitalization effort. I rounded one of the corners of the massive facility and heard a familiar voice. Humbly but forcefully, he was giving directions to a group of about twenty volunteers who had been tasked with shaping up one of the school's outside court-yards. Among the group of volunteers were local business leaders, some engineers, a group of auto body shop workers, and a few members of a college sports team. They were all hanging on every word of instruction from their site leader . . . my nineteen-year-old son, Caleb. Caleb has always been a great kid and a leader type, but to see him in that role made my jaw drop. He barely had time to say hello to dear old dad as he passionately served and supplied each volunteer with what they needed to do their job that day.

Caleb has never been the expressive type when it comes to faith. He never belted out the songs in worship and generally recoils at the touchy-feely aspects of Christianity. But on that job site that day, Caleb demonstrated Christlike love through his volunteer leadership. And I was reminded not only of my love and pride for my kid, but of the powerful role ServErie has played in our ability to equip and unleash volunteers and then see the process repeated. It was awesome to see my own son in that ever-flowing river.

ServErie started in 2008 with seventy-five volunteers on a Saturday morning who were mobilized to be the hands and feet of Jesus in our city. Since then, thousands of volunteers have served and over a hundred churches and organizations have mobilized to help with critical needs in the Erie community. Not only is the boots-on-the-ground manpower fueled by volunteers, but most of the movement's leadership is also run by high-capacity volunteers. It's not unusual for ServErie to mobilize three hundred volunteers on a Saturday to twenty different worksites. Building porches, painting fences, cleaning up entire city blocks, partnering with local nonprofits to help their residents with various projects. Each worksite has been scoped out in advance by site leaders. They analyze the number of volunteers necessary, the required skills, equipment and resources that are needed to get the job done, and any other site-specific challenges that might need to be addressed. These site leaders then mobilize a work team on ServErie days to accomplish the task. Each of those site leaders is (you guessed it) a high-capacity volunteer.

Site leaders will often work with local high school sports teams, businesses who encourage their employees to volunteer, members of local churches, and clients from the various nonprofits who are being served. The entire organizational structure of ServErie has been built on volunteer leadership. Often site leaders will find their replacement and then move on to become project leaders. And then project leaders will find their replacement and move on to become initiative leaders. The current chairwoman of ServErie's board has been involved from the very beginning and has held just about every leadership role in the organization as a high-capacity volunteer. Because of its ability to equip, unleash, and repeat, ServErie has grown and expanded exponentially since 2008. It has become a leader in community revitalization and a powerful force for good in the entire region. What started as a group of volunteers serving on Saturday mornings has grown into expansive renovation projects for low-income schools and revitalization for entire forgotten neighborhoods. Not just our church, but now our city is beginning to experience transformation because of high-capacity volunteers who have committed themselves to the process of equip, unleash, repeat. I want to introduce you to one of those volunteers.

Meet Lisa

Lisa

Lisa's "real" job: Director of Contact Center Operations at Erie Insurance (a Fortune 500 company). She leads a team of 200 Employees handling over 1.5 million calls from customers and agents.

Lisa's volunteer role: She is currently the ServErie Board Chair and has served on the board since the nonprofit was established. She has been involved with ServErie since it began in 2008. She was the Volunteer Coordinator from 2009 to 2016, and the Lead for ServErie Saturday and then Summer Projects from 2017 to 2019.

How did you find your way into this role? "In 2008, I was approached and invited to help with the research and planning of an exciting community volunteer 'program' that was launching from Grace. Prior to this, I had volunteered at Grace in many other roles. Members of the staff knew my skill set and what I was passionate about, so when I was approached, I knew it would be a good fit. I was invited to lunch, where the opportunity was explained in detail. We discussed my role and the time commitment. Over the years, Grace leaders routinely checked in with me to make sure I was feeling comfortable with the time commitment. Based on the volunteer culture we have at Grace as ongoing challenges from the Bible, I always felt a sense of responsibility in my faith to engage in volunteering."

What is energizing about your volunteer role? "I am energized for many reasons. Much of what I get to do is right in my wheelhouse, and it allows me to feel like I am adding value to the team. But I have also had the opportunity to learn new skills. I get to serve with so many amazing people that I didn't know before and probably would have never met had it not been for ServErie. Maybe most energizing is that I have been given the opportunity to honor what Christ has asked of all of us: to be servants in our communities."

What has made you feel like you were a part of staff and not "just" a volunteer? "My thoughts and opinions have always been sought after and valued. I was invited to participate in staff meetings, and I was included in critical information that was pertinent to my service even if it was highly sensitive or confidential."

Talk about a time when being "not paid" got in the way of what you were trying to do. "I don't feel it has. I feel like my opinion is valued equally to the paid staff. The importance of Grace's volunteer culture is not just felt by and respected by Derek; it permeates the entire staff and congregation. Because of that, the paid staff equally values high-capacity volunteers and recognizes that our church would not run as well as it does without both types of leaders."

What advice would you give to other people who may be considering a high-capacity volunteer role? "Pray about it first and make sure it is what God is calling you to. Discuss honestly with your family what the time commitment will be and the potential change to your home life. If your family is not on board, consider this may not be the right time."

Conclusion

One of my motivations in writing this book is to share with other leaders what we've been through in this journey of empowering high-capacity volunteers. And to share it before we have it all figured out, so that, even in all its messiness, others can take this idea to the next level. Remember, Grace Church is about 130 years old. We've accomplished a lot, but it's been like turning an aircraft carrier that doesn't turn on a dime. Most of what has been condensed into a few paragraphs in a chapter of this book represents years of difficult maneuvering —people getting angry, people leaving the church, me messing it up and sometimes our staff repeating mistakes from the past. But maybe someone who is reading this is operating a speedboat instead of an aircraft carrier. For someone starting a church from scratch using this concept of volunteer leadership, the possibilities are endless.

I've often wondered about the volunteer leadership culture's full potential. Could it be possible in our modern times to build a large and influential church with zero paid staff? Or how might God be positioning his church in America for a more decentralized future using a model like this? One that is built less around facilities and services and more on empowerment and neighborhood influence through high-capacity volunteers? COVID-19 has provided the perfect testing ground for new innovation in this area. The whole world has become acclimated to the idea that "church" can happen in a living room. What if churches could reach and disciple and equip and unleash people from afar without any of the trappings of physical space, so that local churches under the leadership of empowered volunteer pastors could spring up in the oddest of places?

How might the gospel penetrate companies and workplaces across our country if more Christians were emboldened and empowered in their spiritual leadership using these principles? I believe that we're only scratching the surface at Grace. We haven't fully jumped into these waters with both feet. I'm hoping that someone reading this book will take the baton and run the next leg of the race.

I remain convinced that the greatest untapped resource in today's church is high-capacity volunteer leaders. And in many churches, they remain available but not used. They are ready to attempt great things for God, to dream big dreams, and accomplish history-altering enterprises. So, pastor, for the sake of the kingdom, *please tap* them. It's time. May we chase God's dream together—an army of ministers, paid and unpaid, empowered to overwhelm the world with the good news of the great love of God.

Notes

Chapter 1

1. "Untapped," *Merriam-Webster's Learner's Dictionary,* accessed June 7, 2020, http://www.learnersdictionary.com/definition/untapped.

2. T. Morgan, *The Unstuck Church Report: Benchmarks + Trends In U.S. Churches,* The Unstuck Group | Church Consulting, Leadership Coaching, accessed June 7, 2020, https://theunstuckgroup.com/trends.

Chapter 2

3. T. Rainer and E. Geiger, *Simple Church* (Nashville: B & H Publishing Group, 2014).

Chapter 3

4. G. Lopez, "Why Incompetent People Often Think They're Actually the Best," *Vox,* accessed June 7, 2020, https://www.vox.com/science-and-health/2017/11/18/16670576/dunning-kruger-effect-video.

5. M. Leary, *The Curse of the Self: Self-Awareness, Egotism, and the Quality of Human Life* (New York: Oxford University Press, 2004), 57–58.

6. A. Hirsch, "What Is APEST?" accessed June 7, 2020, http://www.theforgottenways.org/what-is-apest.aspx.

7. A. Earls, "Majority of American Churches Fall Below 100 In Worship Attendance," Lifeway Research, Feb. 24, 2016, https://lifewayresearch.com/2016/02/24/majority-of-american-churches-fall-below-100-in-worship-attendance.

8. B. Hybels, "The Y Factor," *Christianity Today*, July 11, 2007, https://www.christianitytoday.com/pastors/2007/july-online-only/le-2003-001-10.74.html.

Chapter 4

9. Timothy J. Wengert, "The Priesthood of All Believers and Other Pious Myths," *Institute of Liturgical Studies Occasional Papers*, 117 (2006), https://scholar.valpo.edu/ils_papers/117.

10. M. Luther and E. Plass, *What Luther Says* (St. Louis: Concordia, 1959), 1140.

11. S. Roberts, "McDonald's Opened Their First Restaurant In 1940; Here's The Original Menu," *The Sun*, Sept. 14, 2017, https://www.thesun.co.uk/fabulous/food/3564107/mcdonalds-original-menu-1940-first-ever.

Chapter 5

12. G. Procee, "Revivals In North America: The Great Revival of 1857 In New York," accessed June 7, 2020, http://reformedresource.net/index.php/worldviews/the-hand-of-god-in-history/123-revivals-in-north-america-the-great-revival-of-1857-in-new-york.html.

13. Quoted in "Revival Born in a Prayer Meeting," *Knowing & Doing*, C. S. Lewis Institute, Fall 2004, https://www.cslewisinstitute.org/webfm_send/577.

14. D. Im, "Trend #2 for the Future of Church Planting—Bivocational Ministry," The Exchange with Ed Stetzer, *Christianity Today*, Feb. 9, 2016, https://www.christianitytoday.com/edstetzer/2016/february/trend-2-for-future-of-church-planting-bivocational-ministry.html.

15. E. Stetzer, "Bivocational Ministry As an Evangelism Opportunity," The Exchange with Ed Stetzer, *Christianity Today*, Oct. 15, 2017, https://www.christianitytoday.com/edstetzer/2017/september/bivocational-ministry-as-evangelism-opportunity.html.

16. J. D. Greear, "Determining Your Calling," accessed June 7, 2020, https://jdgreear.com/wp-content/uploads/2012/01/2012.01-Determining-Your-Calling-JD-Greear.pdf.

17. S. Neill and O. Chadwick, *A History of Christian Missions* (New York: Penguin, 1990), 22.

18. G. Lyons, *The Next Christians* (Colorado Springs: Multnomah, 2012), Kindle edition, chap. 7.

Chapter 6

19. C. Groeschel, "It's about Time, Part 2," Craig Groeschel Leadership Podcast, accessed June 7, 2020, https://www.life.church/leadershippodcast/its-about-time-part-2.

Chapter 7

20. Nassim Nicholas Taleb. *Antifragile* (London: Penguin, 2013).

21. Ibid., chap. 2, Kindle.

22. Barna Group, "The State of Pastors," Barna Group in Partnership with Pepperdine University, https://www.barna.com/pastors2017.

23. Carey Nieuwhof, "CNLP 125: David Kinnaman on the Clergy Crisis and State of Pastors Today," Carey Nieuwhof Leadership Podcast, https://careynieuwhof.com/episode125.

Chapter 9

24. Jim Collins, Good to Great (New York: HarperCollins, 2011).

Chapter 11

25. Groeschel, "It's about Time, Part 2."

26. Craig Freudenrich, "How Knights Work," Howstuffworks, https://history.howstuffworks.com/historical-figures/knight3.htm.

27. Larry Osborne, *Sticky Church* (Grand Rapids, MI: Zondervan, 2008), 41–42.

28. Dan Reiland, "The 3-Point Process for Leadership Development," Dan Reiland, February 13, 2017, https://danreiland.com/3-point-process-leadership-development.

Chapter 12

29. Dan Reiland, "Let Your Leaders Lead!" ChurchLeaders.com, December 4, 2015, https://churchleaders.com/pastors/pastor-articles/268031-let-your-leaders-lead.html.

30. Joanne Fritz, "Why You Should Thank Your Volunteers and How to Do It," The Balance Small Business, April 12, 2020. https://www.thebalancesmb.com/creative-ways-to-thank-volunteers-2502573.

31. See B. Blackburn, *Rigor Is Not a Four-letter Word* (New York: Routledge, 2008); M. Reynolds, 2003. *Ten Strategies for Creating a Classroom Culture of High Expectations*

(Atlanta: SREB, 2003); and R. Williamson, and B. Blackburn, *Rigorous Schools and Classrooms: Leading the Way*, https://oregongearup.org/sites/oregongearup.org/files/research-briefs/highexpectations.pdf.

32. American Management Association, "Want More from Your Employees? Raise Your Expectations," January 24, 2019, https://www.amanet.org/articleswant-more-from-your-employees-raise-your-expectations.

33. The seven feasts are Passover (Leviticus 23:4–8), the Feast of Unleavened Bread (Leviticus 23:6), the Feast of First Fruits (Leviticus 23:10), the Feast of Weeks or Pentecost (Leviticus 23:16), the Feast of Trumpets or Rosh Hashanah (Leviticus 23:24), the Day of Atonement or Yom Kippur (Leviticus 16; 23:26–32), and Feast of Tabernacles or Booths (Leviticus 23:34).

34. Marcus Buckingham, "Session Five" (lecture), Global Leadership Summit, Willow Creek Community Church, South Barrington, IL, August 11, 2017.

35. Marcus Buckingham, "Coaching vs. Feedback," Marcus Buckingham, August 11, 2017, https://www.marcusbuckingham.com/rwtb/coaching-vs-feedback/.

36. Buckingham, "Session Five."

37. Robert E. Logan, Sherilyn Carlton, and Tara Miller, *Coaching 101: Discover the Power of Coaching* (St. Charles, IL: ChurchSmart Resources, 2003).

38. Carey Nieuwhof, "5 Healthy Ways to Handle a Difficult Volunteer," CareyNieuwhof.com, July 25, 2019, https://careynieuwhof.com/5-healthy-ways-to-handle-a-difficult-volunteer.

Chapter 13

39. Stanley A. McChrystal, Tantum Collins, David Silverman, and Chris Fussell, *Team of Teams: New Rules of Engagement for a Complex World* (New York: Portfolio/Penguin, 2015), 20.

40. Elijah's story can be found in the Old Testament book of 1 Kings, chapters 17–19.

Connect with Derek Sanford
and access additional resources at
www.dereksanford.com